debbie bliss
EASY
KNITS

debbie bliss

EASY
KNITS

Over 25 simple designs for babies, children and adults

St. Martin's Griffin ≈ *New York*

Dedication:

For Lynda, John, Edward, David, Rob and Mia.

www.stmartins.com

ISBN 0-312-29014-4

Editor: Emma Callery
Designer: Christine Wood
Photographer: Craig Fordham
Stylist: Jemima Mills
Charts and diagrams: Antony Duke

First published in Great Britain by Ebury Press, Random House UK Limited
First U.S. Edition: January 2002

10 9 8 7 6 5 4 3 2 1

Color separation by Colorlito in Milan
Printed and bound in Singapore

CONTENTS

Introduction

Easy Knits is a collection of simple hand knits for adults and children: easy knitting, easy wearing, easy living. From soft, draped cardigans to crisp cotton styles, the accent here is on the detailing – a flash of bright colour in a Fair Isle band or neat moss stitch collar and cuffs. Most of the designs in Easy Knits are within the grasp of the fairly inexperienced knitter, even the colourwork is kept as uncomplicated as possible and I have used good quality yarns that show and emphasize stitch detail in a variety of beautiful shades from neutrals to brights. For the perfect antidote to the stresses of modern life, first choose your style, then pick up your needles and relax.

Basic information

FOLLOWING PATTERN INSTRUCTIONS

Figures for larger sizes are given in round ( ) brackets. Where only one figure appears, this applies to all sizes. Work figures given in square [ ] brackets the number of times stated afterwards. Where 0 appears, no stitches or rows are worked for this size. As you follow the pattern, make sure that you are consistently using the right stitches for your size – it is only too easy to switch sizes inside the brackets. One way to avoid this is to go through the instructions first and mark the size you are knitting with a coloured pen or highlighter.

The quantities of yarn quoted in the instructions are based on the yarn used by the knitter for the original garment and amounts should therefore be considered approximate. A slight variation in tension can make the difference between using less or more yarn than that stated in the pattern. Before buying yarn, look at the measurements on the knitting instructions to be sure what size you want to knit. My patterns quote the actual finished knitted size of the garment rather than just the bust/chest measurements of the wearer. The actual measurements will tell you the width around the whole garment and this will tell you how much ease a garment has; whether it is a generous, baggy style or slim fitting. If you wish to make up the design with less or more ease, you may just need to knit the size smaller or larger size quoted. If you are unsure, measure an existing garment. The length of the garment is usually taken from the shoulder shaping to the cast-on edge.

TENSION

Each pattern in this book specifies a tension – the number of stitches and rows per centimetre/inch that should be obtained with the given needles, yarn and stitch pattern. Check your tension carefully before commencing work.

Use the same yarn, needles and stitch pattern as those to be used for the main work and knit a sample at least 12.5cm/5in square. Smooth out the finished sample on a flat surface, but do not stretch it. To check the tension, place a ruler horizontally on he sample and mark 10cm/4in across with pins. Count the number of stitches between the pins. To check the row tension, place a ruler vertically on the sample and mark 10cm/4in with pins. Count the number of rows between the pins. If the number of stitches and rows is greater than specified, try again using larger needles; if less, use smaller needles. The stitch tension is the most important element to get right.

BUYING YARN FOR A KNITTING PATTERN

Always try to buy the yarn specified in your knitting pattern; however, if you use a substitute, buy a yarn that is the same weight and has the same tension and, where possible, the same fibre content. If you use a synthetic yarn instead of a natural fibre, or even wool where cotton had been originally used, the stitch patterns may appear softer and less delineated. Synthetics can also appear limp, which means that the crispness of the original garment will have been lost. It is essential to check metreage or yardage. Yarn that weighs the same may have different lengths, and you may need to buy more or less yarn.

Check the ball band on the yarn. Most yarn labels now carry all the information you need about fibre content, washing instructions, weight and metreage or yardage. Some of them will tell you the knitting needle sizes to use and the standard tension (or stitch size) these create.

It is essential to check the dye lot number on the yarn label. Yarns are dyed in batches or lots, which can sometimes vary quite considerably. Your retailer may not have the same dye lot later on, so try and buy all your yarn for a project at the same time. If you know that sometimes you require extra yarn to that quoted in a pattern, buy more. If it is not possible to buy the amount you need all in one dye lot, work the borders on the lower edges or the neckband in the odd one, since the colour change is less likely to show here.

The following descriptions of the yarns used in the book are guides to the yarn weights and types:

Debbie Bliss merino double knitting: a 100% merino wool in a double knitting weight. Approximately 110m/50g ball.
Debbie Bliss merino aran: a 100% merino wool in an aran or fisherman yarn. Approximately 78m/50g ball.
Debbie Bliss wool/cotton: a 50% merino wool, 50% cotton lightweight yarn. Approximately 107m/50g ball.
Novita Mohair: an 80% kid mohair, 20% polyamide double knitting yarn. Approximately 200m/50g ball.
Novita Isoveli: a 75% wool, 25% polyamide chunky weight yarn. Approximately 130m/100g ball.
Novita Alpaca: a 100% alpaca double knitting weight yarn. Approximately 103m/50g ball.
Jaeger Cashmina 4 ply: a 4-ply, 80% cashmere, 20% extra-fine merino. Approximately 125m/25g ball.
Jaeger Silk 4 ply: a 4-ply, 100% silk yarn. Approximately 186m/50g ball.
Rowan Spun Double Knitting: a 100% wool double knitting weight. Approximately 200m/50g hank.

WASHING AND DRYING YOUR KNITTING

Check the ball band on your yarn for washing instructions. Many yarns can now be machine washed on a delicate wool cycle. You may find it helpful to make a note of the measurements of the garment, such as the width and length, prior to washing. After washing, lay the garment flat and check the measurements again to see if they are the same. If not, smooth and pat it back into shape.

Natural fibres are usually best hand washed, even if the ball band says otherwise. I find that after successive machine washes, cotton in particular can become rather hard. Use soap flakes specially created for hand knits, and warm rather than hot water. Handle the knits gently in the water – do not rub or wring because this can felt the fabric. Rinse well to get rid of any soap, and squeeze out excess water. You may need to get rid of more water by rolling the garment in a towel, or you can use the delicate spin cycle of the washing machine. Dry the garment by laying it out flat on top of a towel to absorb moisture, smooth and pat into shape. Do not dry knits near direct heat such as a radiator.

Store your knits loosely folded to allow the air to circulate.

KNITTING TERMS

A few specific knitting terms may be unfamiliar to some readers. The list below explains the abbreviations used in this book to help the reader understand how to follow the various stitches and stages.

alt = alternate
beg = begin(ning)
cont = continu(e)(ing)
cm = centimetre(s)
dec = decrease(e)(ing)
foll = follow(ing)
g = gram(mes)
in = inch(es)
inc = increas(e)(ing)
inc one = increase one st by working into the front and back of the stitch
k = knit
m1 = make one by picking up the loop lying between the stitch just worked and next stitch and working into the back of it
mm = millimetre(s)
patt = pattern
p = purl
psso = pass slipped stitch over
rem = remain(ing)
rep = repeat(ing)
skpo = slip one, knit one, pass slipped stitch over
sl = slip
st(s) = stitch(es)
st st = stocking stitch
tbl = through back of loop(s)
tog = together
yb = yarn back
yf = yarn forward
yon = yarn over needle
yrn = yarn around needle

The following terms may be unfamiliar to US readers

UK terms	US terms
Aran wool	'fisherman' yarn
ball band	yarn wrapper
cast off	bind off
DK wool	a yarn between sport and worsted
make up (garment)	finish (garment)
moss stitch	seed stitch
rib	ribbing
stocking stitch	stockinette stitch
tension	gauge
welt	lower borders on sweater front and back

Baby's Cotton Jacket with Tie Bow and Bootees

MATERIALS
Jacket 4(4:5) 50g balls of Debbie Bliss wool/cotton.
Bootees One 50g ball of Debbie Bliss wool/cotton.
Pair each of 3mm (No 11/US 2) and 3¼mm (No 10/US 3) knitting needles.
1 button.

MEASUREMENTS

To fit age	3-6	6-9	9-12	months
Actual chest measurement	60	63	66	cm
	23½	25	26	in
Length	24	26	28	cm
	9½	10 ¼	11	in
Sleeve length	14	16	18	cm
	5½	6¼	7	in

TENSION
25 sts and 34 rows to 10cm/4in square over st st on 3¼mm (No 10/US 3) needles.

ABBREVIATIONS
See page 7.

Jacket
BACK AND FRONTS
With 3mm (No 11/US 2) needles cast on 153(161:169) sts.
Moss st row K1, * p1, k1; rep from * to end.
Rep last row 5 times more.
Change to 3¼mm (No 10/US 3) needles.
Next row Moss st 5, k to last 5 sts, moss st 5.
Next row Moss st 5, p to last 5 sts, moss st 5.
Cont in st st with moss st borders until work measures 13(14:15)cm/5¼(5½:5¾)in from beg, ending with a k row.
Left Front
Next row Moss st 5, p34(36:38), turn.
Work on this set of sts only until left front measures 20(22:23)cm/8(8¾:9)in from beg, ending at front edge.
Shape Neck
Next row Moss st 5, p4, leave these sts on a safety pin, p to end. 30(32:34) sts.
Dec one st at neck edge on every row until 22(23:24) sts rem.
Cont straight until work measures 24(26:28)cm/9½(10¼:11)in from beg, ending at armhole edge.
Shape Shoulder
Cast off 11(11:12) sts at beg of next row.
Work 1 row.
Cast off rem 11(12:12) sts.

BACK
With wrong side facing, join on yarn, p75(79:83), turn.
Work on this set of sts only until back measures same as left front to shoulder shaping, ending with a p row.
Shape Shoulders
Cast off 11(11:12) sts at beg of next 2 rows and 11(12:12) sts at beg of foll 2 rows.
Leave rem 31(33:35) sts on a holder.
Right Front
With wrong side facing, rejoin yarn to rem sts, p to last 5 sts, moss st 5. 39(41:43) sts.
Complete to match left front.

SLEEVES
With 3mm (No 11/US 2) needles cast on 33(37:41) sts.
Moss st 6 rows as given for Back and Fronts.
Change to 3¼mm (No 10/US 3) needles.
Beg with a k row, work in st st, inc one st at each end of the next and every foll 4th row until there are 53(57:61) sts.
Cont straight until sleeve measures 14(16:18)cm/5½(6¼:7)in from beg, ending with a p row.
Cast off.

NECKBAND
Join shoulder seams.
With 3mm (No 11/US 2) needles and right side facing, slip 9 sts from right front safety pin onto a needle, pick up and k15 sts up right side of front neck, k31(33:35) sts from back neck, pick up and k15 sts down left side of front neck, k4, moss st 5 sts on left front safety pin. 79(81:83) sts.
Moss st 2 rows.
Buttonhole row Moss st 2, work 2tog, yf, moss st to end.
Moss st 2 rows.
Next row Moss st 5, cast off rem sts.
With wrong side facing, rejoin yarn to rem sts, moss st to end.
Moss st a further 5 rows.
Cast off.

BOWS (make 2)
With 3¼mm (No 10/US 3) needles cast on 6 sts.
Beg with a k row, work in st st for 2 rows.
Next row K1, [m1, k1] 5 times. 11 sts.
Work 24 rows moss st.
Cast off.

TO MAKE UP
Join together cast-on edges of bows. Sew bow to neckband at centre of right front. Fold neckband extension over centre of bow and sew cast-off edge in place. Sew button on back of right front neckband to match buttonhole. Sew on sleeves. Join sleeve seams.

Bootees (make 2)

TO MAKE

With 3¼mm (No 10/US 3) needles cast on 40 sts.

K 1 row.

Inc row P twice in first st, p18, p twice in each of next 2 sts, p18, p twice in last st.

K 1 row.

Inc row P twice in first st, p20, p twice in each of next 2 sts, p20, p twice in last st.

K 1 row.

Inc row P twice in first st, p22, p twice in each of next 2 sts, p22, p twice in last st.

K 1 row. 52 sts.

Work 6 rows in st st.

Shape Instep

Next row K30, skpo, turn.

Next row P9, p2tog, turn.

Next row K9, skpo, turn.

Rep last 2 rows 7 times more, then the first of the 2 rows again.

Next row K to end. 34 sts.

Work 6 rows moss st.

Next row Cast off 15 sts, moss st next 3 sts, cast off rem 15 sts.

With wrong side facing, rejoin yarn to rem 4 sts, moss st to end.

Moss st a further 5 rows.

Cast off.

BOWS (make 4)

With 3¼mm (No 10/US 3) needles cast on 5 sts.

Beg with a k row, work in st st for 2 rows.

Next row K1, [m1, k1] 4 times. 9 sts.

Work 12 rows moss st.

Cast off.

TO MAKE UP

Join together cast-on edges of bows. Sew bow to moss st band at centre. Fold extension over centre of bow and sew cast-off edge in place. Join back heel and sole seam.

Double-breasted Moss Stitch Jacket and Hat

MATERIALS
Jacket 8(8:9) 50g balls of Debbie Bliss merino aran.
Hat Two 50g balls of Debbie Bliss merino/aran.
Pair each of 3¾mm (No 9/US 4), 4½mm (No 7/US 7) and 5mm (No 6/US 8) knitting needles.
8 buttons.

MEASUREMENTS
Jacket

To fit ages	1	2	3	years
Actual chest measurement	70	74	79	cm
	27½	29	31	in
Length	35	39	43	cm
	13¾	15½	17	in
Sleeve length	20	22	25	cm
(with cuff turned back)	8	8½	9¾	in

Hat

To fit	1-3 years

TENSION
18 sts and 32 rows to 10cm/4in square over moss st on 5mm (No 6/US 8) needles.

ABBREVIATIONS
See page 7.

Jacket
BACK
With 5mm (No 6/US 8) needles cast on 65(69:73) sts.
1st row (right side) K1, * p1, k1; rep from * to end.
This row forms the moss st patt.
Cont in moss st until back measures 35(39:43)cm/13¾(15½:17)in from beg, ending with a wrong-side row.
Shape Shoulders
Cast off 11(12:13) sts at beg of next 2 rows and 12(12:13) sts at beg of next 2 rows.
Cast off rem 19(21:21) sts.

POCKET LININGS (make 2)
With 5mm (No 6/US 8) needles cast on 15(17:19) sts.
Work 11(12:13)cm/4¼(4¾:5¼)in in moss st.
Leave sts on a spare needle.

LEFT FRONT
With 5mm (No 6/US 8) needles cast on 43(45:47) sts.
Cont in moss st until front measures 13(14:15)cm/5(5½:6)in from beg, ending with a wrong-side row.

Place Pocket

Next row Moss st 6, cast off next 15(17:19) sts, moss st to end.

Next row Moss st 22, work across sts of one pocket lining, moss st to end.

Cont in moss st until front measures 30(34:38)cm/11¾(13½:15)in from beg, ending with a right-side row.

Shape Neck

Cast off 15(16:17) sts at beg of next row.

Dec one st at neck edge on every row until 23(24:26) sts rem.

Cont straight until front measures same as Back to shoulder, ending at side edge.

Shape Shoulder

Cast off 11(12:13) sts at beg of next row.

Work 1 row.

Cast off rem 12(12:13) sts.

RIGHT FRONT

With 5mm (No 6/US 8) needles cast on 43(45:47) sts.

Cont in moss st until front measures 13(14:15)cm/5(5½:6)in from beg, ending with a wrong-side row.

Place Pocket

Next row Moss st 22, cast off next 15(17:19) sts, moss st to end.

Next row Moss st 6, work across sts of one pocket lining, moss st to end.

Cont in patt until front measures 14(15:16)cm/5½(6:6¼)in from beg, ending with a wrong-side row.

Buttonhole row Moss st 3, yf, work 2tog, moss st 10, yf, work 2tog, moss st to end.

Cont in patt until front measures 21.5(24:26.5)cm/8½(9½:10½)in from beg, ending with a wrong-side row.

Work the buttonhole row again.

Cont in patt until front measures 29(33:37)cm/11½(13:14½)in from beg, ending with a wrong-side row.

Work the buttonhole row again.

Cont in moss st until front measures 30(34:38)cm/11¾(13½:15)in from beg, ending with a wrong-side row.

Shape Neck

Cast off 15(16:17) sts at beg of next row.

Dec one st at neck edge on every row until 23(24:26) sts rem.

Cont straight until front measures same as Back to shoulder, ending at side edge.

Shape Shoulder

Cast off 11(12:13) sts at beg of next row.

Work 1 row.

Cast off rem 12(12:13) sts.

SLEEVES

With 5mm (No 6/ US 8) needles cast on 35(39:43) sts.

Work 5(6:7)cm/2(2½:2¾)in in moss st.

Change to 4½mm (No 7/US 7) needles.

Work 5(6:7)cm/2(2½:2¾)in in moss st.

Change to 5mm (No 6/US 8) needles.

Cont in moss st and inc one st at each end of the 3rd and every foll 4th row until there are 55(61:67) sts.

Cont straight until sleeve measures 25(28:32)cm/10(11:12½)in from beg.

Cast off.

COLLAR

Join shoulder seams.

With 3¾mm (No 9/US 4) needles and right side facing, miss first cast-off 10 sts, pick up and k5(6:7) sts from rem cast-off sts, 18 sts up left side of front, 19(21:21) sts across back neck, 18 sts down right side of front neck, 5(6:7) sts from first cast-off sts. 65(69:71) sts.

Next row Moss st to end.

Next 2 rows Moss st to last 5(6:7) sts, turn.

Next 2 rows Moss st to last 8(9:10) sts, turn.

Next 2 rows Moss st to last 11(12:13) sts, turn.

Next 2 rows Moss st to last 14(15:16) sts, turn.

Next 2 rows Moss st to last 17(18:19) sts, turn.

Next 2 rows Moss st to last 20(21:22) sts, turn.

Moss st to end.

Work 18 rows moss st. Cast off.

BACK BELT

With 3¾mm (No 9/US 4) needles cast on 49(53:55) sts.

Work 2.5cm/1in in moss st. Cast off.

TO MAKE UP

Sew on sleeves. Join side and sleeve seams reversing seam on last 7(8:9)cm/2¾(3:3½)in of cuff. Sew down pocket linings. Sew on buttons. Secure belt in place with buttons.

Hat

TO MAKE

Using 4½mm (No 7/US 7) needles cast on 80 sts.

Rib row * K1, p1; rep from * to end.

Rep the last row 4 times more.

Inc row K2, * m1, k3, m1, k2; rep from * to last 3 sts, m1, k3. 111 sts.

Change to 5mm (No 6/US 8) needles.

Cont in moss st until work measures 10cm/4in from beg.

Shape Top

Dec row K1, * work 3tog, moss st 19; rep from * to end. Moss st 1 row.

Dec row K1, * work 3tog, moss st 17; rep from * to end. Moss st 1 row.

Dec row K1, * work 3tog, moss st 15; rep from * to end. Moss st 1 row.

Cont in this way dec 10 sts on every alt row until 11 sts rem. Moss st 1 row.

Break off yarn thread through rem sts, pull up and secure. Join seam.

Striped Scarf

MATERIALS
Two 50g balls each of Debbie Bliss merino double knitting in
Brown (A) and Light Pink (B).
One ball each of same in Rust (C) and Fuchsia Pink (D).
Pair of 4mm (No 8/US 6) knitting needles.
Long circular 4mm (No 8/US 6) knitting needle.

MEASUREMENTS
Scarf measures 14cm x 109cm/5½in x 43in.

TENSION
41 sts and 28 rows to 10cm/4in square over rib patt on 4mm
(No 8/US 6) needles.

ABBREVIATIONS
See page 7.

TO MAKE
With 4mm (No 8/US 6) needles and A, cast on 58 sts.
1st rib row K2, * p2, k2; rep from * to end.
2nd rib row P2, * k2, p2; rep from * to end.
These 2 rows form the rib patt.
Cont in rib and stripe patt as folls:
9 rows A, 2 rows D, 2 rows A, 2 rows C, 1 row A, 4 rows B, 1 row
D, 1 row C, 9 rows B, 1 row D, 2 rows B, 2 rows A, 1 row D, 1
row A, 2 rows C, 1 row A, 1 row D, 10 rows A, 11 rows B, 1 row
D, 1 row C, 1 row B, 1 row D, 3 rows B, 4 rows A, [1 row C, 1
row A] twice, 2 rows D, 8 rows A, 6 rows B, 1 row C, 1 row B, 2
rows D, 1 row B, 1 row C, 6 rows B, 2 rows A, 2 rows C, 10 rows
A, 2 rows D, 2 rows A, 5 rows B, 1 row C, 1 row D, 2 rows B, 1
row D, 8 rows B, 5 rows A, 1 row D, 2 rows A, 1 row C – the last
row is the centre of the scarf, now work stripe patt in reverse
order.
Using A, work 2 more rows, cast off.

EDGINGS (both sides alike)
With wrong side facing and using circular 4mm (No 8/US 6)
needle, pick up and k224 sts along side edge.
Beg with a p row, work 3 rows st st.
Cast off.

TO COMPLETE
Fold edgings to right side, stitch cast-off edge in place, encasing
ends. Make 2 pompoms each in B and D and 1 each A and C.
Sew 3 pompoms to each short end.

Dress with Fair Isle Border

MATERIALS

4(4) 50g balls Rowan Spun Double Knitting in Main Colour (M)
1 ball each of Rowan Wool Cotton in Blue (B), Cream (C), Red (D),
Pink (E) and Oatmeal (F).
Pair of 4mm (No 8/US 6) knitting needles.
1 short 3¼mm(No 10/US 3) circular knitting needle.
1 button.

MEASUREMENTS

To fit	18-24	24-36	months
Actual chest measurement	62	67	cm
	24½	26½	in
Length	40	45	cm
	15¾	17¾	in
Sleeve length	22	24	cm
	8¾	9½	in

TENSION

21 sts and 30 rows to 10cm/4in square over st st on 4mm
(No 8/US 6) needles.

ABBREVIATIONS

See page 7.

NOTE

Read chart from right to left on right side rows and from left to right
on wrong side rows. When working in pattern, strand yarn not in
use loosely across wrong side to keep fabric elastic.

BACK

With 4mm (No 8/US 6) needles and M, cast on 87(87) sts.
Beg with a k row, work 6 rows in st st.
Join on B.
Using B, k 2 rows to form hemline.
Cut off B. Cont in M.
Beg with a k row, work 10 rows in st st.
Work in patt from Chart until 13 rows of Chart have been worked.
Cont in M and st st, **at the same time** dec one st at each end of
the next and every foll 5th(6th) row until 67(73) sts rem.
Work straight until back measures 28(32)cm/11(12½)in from
hemline, ending with a p row.

Shape Armholes

Cast off 4 sts at beg of next 2 rows.
Dec one st at each end of the next and every foll alt row until
45(49) sts rem, ending with a p row.

Back Opening

Next row K21(23) sts, turn and work on these sts for first side of
back opening.
Next row Cast on 3 sts, p to end.
Beg with a k row, work 12(14) rows in st st.

Shape Neck

Next row K to last 8(9) sts, leave these sts on a holder, turn.
Next row Cast off 3 sts, p to end.
K 1 row.
Next row Cast off 2 sts, p to end.
Beg with a k row, work 2 rows in st st.

Shape Shoulder

Cast off 5(6) sts at beg of next row.
P 1 row.
Cast off rem 6 sts.

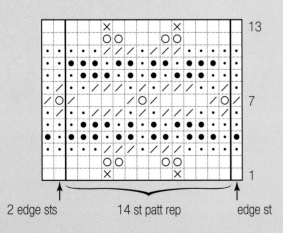

2 edge sts   14 st patt rep   edge st

Key

☐ Main Colour (M)	⊙ Red
· Blue	╱ Cream
☒ Pink	● Oatmeal

With right side facing, rejoin yarn to rem sts, k to end.
Beg with a p row, work 9(11) rows in st st.
Buttonhole row K2, yf, k2tog, k to end.
Beg with a p row, work 3 rows in st st.
Shape Neck
Next row K 8(9) sts, leave these sts on a holder, k to end.
P 1 row.
Next row Cast off 3 sts, k to end.
P 1 row.
Next row Cast off 2 sts, k to end.
Beg with a p row, work 2 rows in st st.
Shape Shoulder
Cast off 5(6) sts at beg of next row.
K 1 row.
Cast off rem 6 sts.

FRONT
Work as given for Back until front measures 36(41)cm/14¼(16 ¼)in from hemline, ending with a p row.
Shape Neck
Next row K16(18) sts, turn and work on these sts for first side of neck shaping.
Cast off 4 sts at beg of next row.
Dec one st at neck edge on every foll alt row until 11(12) sts rem.
Cont without further shaping until front measures same as Back to shoulder, ending at side edge.
Shape Shoulder
Cast off 5(6) sts at beg of next row.
P 1 row.
Cast off rem 6 sts.
With right side facing, slip centre 13 sts onto a holder, rejoin yarn, k to end.
Complete to match first side, reversing shaping.

SLEEVES
With 4mm (No 8/US 6) needles and M, cast on 34(36) sts.
Beg with a k row, work 6 rows in st st.
Join on B.
Using B, k 2 rows to form hemline.
Cut off B. Cont in M.
Beg with a k row, work 10 rows in st st.
Working in st st, inc one st at each end of the next and every foll 5th row until there are 50(54) sts.
Cont straight until sleeve measures 22(24)cm/8¾(9½)in from hemline, ending with a p row.
Shape Top
Cast off 4 sts at beg of next 2 rows.
Dec one st at each end of the next 5 rows, then on 3(4) foll alt rows. Dec one st at each end of every row until 10(12) sts rem.
Cast off.

NECKBAND
Join shoulder seams.
With right side facing and using 3¼mm (No 10/US 3) circular knitting needle and M, slip 8(9) sts from left back onto needle, pick up and k10(11) sts up left back to shoulder, 16(18) sts down left front neck, k across 13 sts from front neck holder, pick up and k16(18) sts up right front neck to shoulder, 10(11) sts from right back neck, k across 8(9) sts on back neck holder. 81(89) sts.
Work backwards and forwards in rows as follows:
Beg with a p row, work 3 rows in st st.
Join on B.
Using B, k 2 rows to form hemline.
Cut off B. Cont in M.
Beg with a k row, work 4 rows in st st.
Cast off in rib

TO MAKE UP
Sew on sleeves. Join side and sleeve seams. Fold all hems to wrong side and slip stitch in place. Sew on button.

Fair Isle Jacket

MATERIALS
4(6:6) 50g balls of Debbie Bliss wool/cotton in Main Colour (M).
1 ball each of same in Navy, Lilac, Aqua, Cream, Pink, Dark Red
and Yellow.
Pair each of 3mm (No11/US 2) and 3¼mm (No 10/US 3) knitting
needles.
Long circular 3mm (No11/US 2) and 3¼mm (No 10/US 3) knitting
needle.
25(30:35)cm/10(12:13¾)in open-ended zip.

MEASUREMENTS

To fit ages	1	2	3	years
Actual chest measurement	66	73	82	cm
	26	28¾	32¼	in
Length	33	37	41	cm
	13	14½	16	in
Sleeve length	20	23	26	cm
	8	9	10¼	in

TENSION
26 sts and 30 rows to 10cm/4in square over patt on 3¼mm
(No 10/US 3) needles.

ABBREVIATIONS
See page 7.

NOTE
Read chart from right to left on right side rows and from left to right
on wrong side rows. When working in pattern, strand yarn not in
use loosely across wrong side to keep fabric elastic.

BACK AND FRONTS
With 3mm (No11/US 2) circular needle and M, cast on
175(191:215) sts.
Work backwards and forwards in rows as follows:
Moss st row K1, * p1, k1; rep from * to end.
Rep last row 4 times more.
Change to 3¼mm (No 10/US 3) circular needle.
Work in patt as folls:
1st row (right side) Using M, moss st 3, work across 8 sts of Chart
to last 4 sts, work edge st, using M, moss st 3.
2nd row Using M, moss st 3, work edge st, work across 8 sts of
Chart to last 3 sts, using M, moss st 3.
These 2 rows set the Fair Isle patt.
Cont in patt with moss st borders until work measures
19(22:25)cm/7½(8¾:10)in from beg, ending with a wrong-side row.

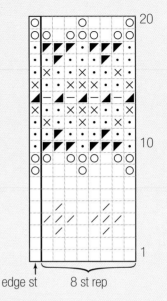

edge st   8 st rep

Key
☐ Dark Red (—)
◼ Yellow
☒ Pink
⦁ Cream
◯ Aqua
⦸ Navy (/)
☐ Main Colour (M)
◣ Lilac

Divide for Back and Fronts

Next row Moss st 3, patt 40(44:50), leave these sts on a holder for right front, patt until there are 89(97:109) sts on needle, leave these sts on a holder for back, patt 40(44:50), moss st 3.

Cont on last set of 43(47:53) sts only for left front.

Work straight until work measures 27(31:35)cm/10½(12¼:13¾)in from beg, ending with a wrong-side row.

Shape Neck

Next row Patt to last 3 sts, leave sts on a holder.

Dec one st at neck edge on every row until 28(30:34) sts rem.

Work 5(3:1) rows straight, ending at armhole edge.

Shape Shoulder

Cast off 14(15:17) sts at beg of next row.

Work 1 row.

Cast off rem 14(15:17) sts.

With wrong side facing, work across centre 89(97:109) sts for back.

Cont straight until back measures same as Front to shoulder shaping, ending with a wrong-side row.

Shape Shoulders

Cast off 14(15:17) sts at beg of next 4 rows.

Cast off rem 33(37:41) sts.

With wrong side facing, work across last set of 43(47:53) sts for right front.

Complete to match left front.

SLEEVES

Using 3mm (No11/US 2) needles and M, cast on 37(43:49) sts.

Work 4 rows moss st.

Inc row Moss st 2, * m1, moss st 3; rep from * to last 2 sts, m1, moss st 2. 49(57:65) sts.

Change to 3¼mm (No 10/US 3) needles.

Work in patt from Chart **at the same time** inc and work into patt one st at each end of the 3rd and every foll 4th row until there are 73(79:83) sts.

Cont straight until sleeve measures 20(23:26)cm/8(9:10¼)in from beg, ending with a wrong-side row.

Cast off.

RIGHT COLLAR

Join shoulder seams.

With right side facing and using 3mm (No11/US 2) needles and M, slip 3 sts from holder onto a needle, turn, moss st 3.

Cont in moss st **at the same time** inc one st at inside edge, on next and every foll alt row until there are 19 sts. Cont straight until shaped edge fits along shaped edge of jacket to shoulder, ending at straight edge.

Shape Collar

Next 2 rows Moss st 11, turn, sl 1, moss st to end.

Moss st 6 rows.

Rep last 8 rows until the shorter edge fits halfway across back neck sts. Cast off.

LEFT COLLAR

With right side facing and using 3mm (No 11/US 2) needles and M, moss st 3 sts from holder.

Complete to match right collar.

TO MAKE UP

Sew on sleeves. Join sleeve seams. Sew in zip.

Longline Belted Cardigan and Hat

MATERIALS
Jacket and Hat 6(7) 100g balls of Novita Isoveli.
Pair each of 5½mm (No 5/US 9) and 6mm (No 4/US 10) knitting needles.
7 Buttons.

MEASUREMENTS
Cardigan

To fit ages	2-3	4-5	years
Actual chest measurement	90	95	cm
	35¼	37½	in
Length	46	52	cm
	18	20½	in
Sleeve length	24	30	cm
(with cuff turned back)	9½	11¾	in

Hat

To fit ages	2-3	4-5	years

TENSION
16 sts and 22 rows to 10cm/4in square over st st on 6mm (No 4/US 10) needles.

ABBREVIATIONS
See page 7.

Cardigan
BACK
With 6mm (No 4/US 10) needles cast on 74(78) sts.
1st size only
1st row K2, * p2, k2; rep from * to end.
2nd row P2, * k2, p2; rep from * to end.
2nd size only
1st row P2, * k2, p2; rep from * to end.
2nd row K2, * p2, k2; rep from * to end.
Both sizes
Rep last 2 rows 13(15) times more.
Beg with a k row, work in st st for 72(84) rows.
Shape Shoulders
Cast off 12(13) sts at beg of next 2 rows and 13(14) sts at beg of foll 2 rows.
Cast off rem 24(24) sts.

POCKET LININGS (make 2)

With 5½mm (No 5/US 9) needles cast on 22 sts.
1st row K2, * p2, k2; rep from * to end.
2nd row P2, * k2, p2; rep from * to end.
Rep last 2 rows 13(15) times more.
Leave these sts on a holder.

LEFT FRONT

With 6mm (No 4/US 10) needles cast on 43(45) sts.
1st size only
1st row K2, * p2, k2; rep from * to last 5 sts, p2, k3.
2nd row K1, p2, * k2, p2; rep from * to end.
2nd size only
1st row * P2, k2; rep from * to last 5 sts, p2, k3.
2nd row K1, * p2, k2; rep from * to end.
Both sizes
Rep last 2 rows 12(14) times more and 1st row again.
Next row Rib 6, inc in next st, leave these 8 sts on a holder, inc in next st, rib next 5 sts, cast off next 22 sts, rib rem 7(9) sts.
Next row K8(10), k across sts of pocket lining, k7. 37(39) sts.
Beg with a p row, work in st st for 62(70) rows.
Shape Neck
Cast off 6 sts at beg of next row.
Dec one st at neck edge on every row until 25(27) sts rem.
Work straight until front measures same as Back to shoulder, ending at side edge.
Shape Shoulder
Cast off 12(13) sts at beg of next row.
Work 1 row.
Cast off rem 13(14) sts.

RIGHT FRONT

With 6mm (No 4/US 10) needles cast on 43(45) sts.
1st size only
1st row K3, * p2, k2; rep from * to end
2nd row P2, * k2, p2; rep from * to last st, k1.
2nd size only
1st row K3, * p2, k2; rep from * to last 2 sts, p2.
2nd row K2, * p2, k2; rep from * to last 3 sts, p2, k1.
Both sizes
Rep last 2 rows once more.
Buttonhole row K3, p2tog, yrn, rib to end of row.
Rib a further 7(9) rows.
Rep buttonhole row once more.
Rib a further 7(9) rows.
Rep buttonhole row once more.
Rib a further 6(6) rows.
Next row Rib 8(10), cast off next 22 sts, rib next 5 sts, inc in next st, leave rem 7 sts on a holder.
Next row K7, k across sts of pocket lining, k8(10). 37(39) sts.
Beg with a p row, work in st st for 63(71) rows.

Shape Neck

Cast off 6 sts at beg of next row.
Dec one st at neck edge on every row until 25(27) sts rem.
Work straight until front measures same as Back to shoulder, ending at side edge.
Shape Shoulder
Cast off 12(13) sts at beg of next row.
Work 1 row.
Cast off rem 13(14) sts.

SLEEVES

With 6mm (No 4/US 10) needles cast on 30(34) sts.
1st row K2, * p2, k2; rep from * to end.
2nd row P2, * k2, p2; rep from * to end.
Rep last 2 rows 3(4) times more.
Change to 5½mm (No 5/US 9) needles.
Work a further 8(10) rows in rib, inc 6 sts on last row. 36(40) sts.
Change to 6mm (No 4/US 10) needles.
Beg with a k row, work in st st, inc one st at each end of the 3rd and every foll 4th row until there are 56(64) sts.
Cont straight until sleeve measures 28(34)cm/11(13½)in from beg, ending with a p row.
Cast off.

BUTTON BAND

Join shoulder seams.
With 5½mm (No 5/US 9) needles and right side facing, k3, p2, k3 across sts on left front holder.
Next row K1, p2, k2, p2, k1.
Next row K3, p2, k3.
These 2 rows set the rib.
Work a further 59(67) rows.
Leave sts on a holder.

BUTTONHOLE BAND

With 5½mm (No 5/US 9) needles and wrong side facing, inc in first st, p2, k2, p2, k1 across sts on right front holder.
Next row K3, p2, k3.
Next row K1, p2, k2, p2, k1.
These 2 rows set the rib.
Work a further 60(68) rows, working 4 more buttonholes, as before, but now with 15(17) rows between.
Leave sts on a holder, do not break yarn.

COLLAR

Join shoulder seams.
Sew front bands in place.
With 5½mm (No 5/US 9) needles and right side facing, cast off 5 sts, then k rem 2 sts on buttonhole band, pick up and k16(18) sts up right front neck, 21(23) sts from back neck, 16(18) sts down left front neck, k3, p2, k3 from button band. 64(70) sts.

Next row Cast off 5 sts, p1, k1, * p2, k1; rep from * to end. 59(65) sts.

This row sets the rib patt with garter st edge sts.

Next 2 rows Rib to last 20 sts, turn.

Next 2 rows Rib to last 16 sts, turn.

Next 2 rows Rib to last 12 sts, turn.

Next 2 rows Rib to last 8 sts, turn.

Rib to end.

Next row K1, p2, * inc in next st, p2; rep from * to last st, k1.

Next row K3, * p2, k2; rep from * to last 5 sts, p2, k3.

Next row K1, p2, * k2, p2, rep from * to last st, k1.

Rep last 2 rows 4 times more.

Cast off in rib.

BELT

With 5½mm (No 5/US 9) needles cast on 8 sts.

1st row K3, p2, k3.

2nd row K1, p2, k2, p2, k1.

Rep last 2 rows until belt measures 120cm/47¼in from beg, ending with a 2nd row.

Cast off in rib.

TO MAKE UP

Sew on sleeves. Join side and sleeve seams reversing seam for cuff for 4cm/1½in. Sew on buttons. Sew down pocket linings. Make 2 belt carriers on side seam at waist level

Hat

TO MAKE

With 6mm (No 4/US 10) needles cast on 74(78) sts.

1st rib row K2, * p2, k2; rep from * to end.

2nd rib row P2, * k2, p2; rep from * to end.

Rep these 2 rows for 4cm/1½in, ending with a 1st rib row.

Change to 5½mm (No 5/US 9) needles.

Beg with 1st rib row, work in rib for a further 4cm/1½in.

Change to 6mm (No 4/US 10) needles and cont in rib until hat measures 20(24)cm/8(9½)in from beg, ending with a 2nd rib row.

Shape Top

1st row K2, *p2tog, k2; rep from * to end.

2nd row P2, * k1, p2; rep from * to end.

3rd row K2, * p1, k2; rep from * to end.

4th row P2, * k1, p2; rep from * to end.

5th row K2tog, *p1, k2tog; rep from * to end.

6th row P1, * k1, p1; rep from * to end.

7th row K1, * k2tog; rep from * to end.

8th row P1(0), * p2tog; rep from * to end.

Break off yarn, thread end through rem sts, pull up and secure.

Join seam reversing seam on last 4cm/1½in.

Baby Crossover Top and Bootees

MATERIALS

Crossover Top 5(6:7) 25g balls Jaeger Cashmina 4 ply.
Pair each of 3mm (No 11/US 2) and 3¼mm (No 10/US 3) knitting needles.
Bootees One 25g ball Jaeger Cashmere 4 ply.
Pair of 3mm (No 11/US 2) knitting needles for first size or 3¼mm (No 10/US 3) knitting needles for second size.

MEASUREMENTS

Crossover Top

To fit ages	3-6	6-12	12-18	months
Actual chest measurement	54	57	64	cm
	21¼	22½	25¼	in
Length	21	23	25	cm
	8¼	9	10	in
Sleeve length	18	22	24	cm
	7	8½	9½	in

Bootees

To fit	3	6	months

TENSION

28 sts and 36 rows to 10cm/4in square over st st on 3¼mm (No 10/US 3) needles.

ABBREVIATIONS

See page 7.

Top

BACK

With 3mm (No 11/US 2) needles cast on 78(82:92) sts.
K 9 rows.
Change to 3¼mm (No 10/US 3) needles.
Beg with a k row, work 68(76:82) rows in st st.
Shape Shoulders
Cast off 10(11:12) sts at beg of next 4 rows.
Cast off rem 38(38:44) sts.

LEFT FRONT

With 3mm (No 11/US 2) needles cast on 78(82:92) sts.
K 9 rows.
Change to 3¼mm (No 10/US 3) needles.
Next row K to end.
Next row K5, p to end.
Rep last 2 rows 3(5:5) times more and the first row again.
Shape Neck
Next 2 rows K1, sl 1, turn, sl 1, k1.
Next 2 rows K2, sl 1, turn, sl 1, k2.

Next 2 rows K3, sl 1, turn, sl 1, k3.

Next 2 rows K2, sl 1, turn, sl 1, k2.

Next 2 rows K1, sl 1, turn, sl 1, k1.

Next row K5 sts and slip these sts onto a safety pin, p to end.

Next row K to last 3 sts, k2tog, k1.

Next row P1, p2tog, p to end.

Rep last 2 rows until 20(22:24) sts rem.

Work 5(7:5) rows straight.

Shape Shoulder

Cast off 10(11:12) sts at beg of next row.

Work 1 row. Cast off rem 10(11:12) sts.

RIGHT FRONT

With 3mm (No 11/US 2) needles cast on 78(82:92) sts.

K 9 rows.

Change to 3¼mm (No 10/US 3) needles.

Next row K to end.

Next row P to last 5 sts, k5.

Rep last 2 rows 4(6:6) times more.

Shape Neck

Next 2 rows K1, sl 1, turn, sl 1, k1.

Next 2 rows K2, sl 1, turn, sl 1, k2.

Next 2 rows K3, sl 1, turn, sl 1, k3.

Next 2 rows K2, sl 1, turn, sl 1, k2.

Next 2 rows K1, sl 1, turn, sl 1, k1.

Next row K6, sl 1, k1, psso, k to end.

Next row P to last 8 sts, p2tog tbl, p1, slip last 5 sts on a safety pin.

Next row K1, sl 1, k1, psso, k to end.

Next row P to last 3 sts, p2tog tbl, p1.

Rep last 2 rows until 20(22:24) sts rem.

Work 5(7:5) rows straight.

Shape Shoulder

Cast off 10(11:12) sts at beg of next row.

Work 1 row. Cast off rem 10(11:12) sts.

SLEEVES

With 3mm (No 11/US 2) needles cast on 38(42:46) sts.

K 9 rows.

Change to 3¼mm (No 10/US 3) needles.

Beg with a k row, cont in st st **at the same time** inc one st at each end of the 3rd and every foll 6th row until there are 56(64:70) sts. Cont straight until sleeve measures 18(22:24)cm/7(8½:9½)in from beg, ending with a p row. Cast off.

RIGHT COLLAR

Join shoulder seams.

Position right front over left front and place a marker thread on both fronts where they cross.

With right side facing and using 3mm (No 11/US 2) needles, slip 5 sts from safety pin onto a needle, turn, k5.

Cont in garter st (every row k) until band is long enough to fit along neck edge to marker, now inc one st at inside edge, on next and every foll alt row until there are 24 sts. Cont straight until shaped edge fits along shaped edge to shoulder, ending at straight edge.

Shape Collar

Next 2 rows K13, turn, sl 1, k to end.

K 6 rows.

Rep last 8 rows until the shorter edge fits halfway across back neck sts. Cast off.

LEFT COLLAR

With right side facing and using 3mm (No 11/US 2) needles, k5 sts from safety pin, turn k5.

Complete to match right collar.

TIES

With 3mm (No 11/US 2) needles needles cast on 5 sts.

Cont in garter st until tie measures 36(42:48)cm/14¼(16½:19)in. Cast off.

TO MAKE UP

Sew on sleeves. Sew ties to fronts level with neck shaping. Join side and sleeve seams, leaving small opening in right seam level with neck shaping. Join collar seam and sew to neck edge.

Bootees (make 2)

TO MAKE

With 3mm (No 11/US 2) needles **for first size** or 3¼mm (No 10/US 3) needles **for second size** cast on 36 sts.

K 21 rows.

Shape Instep

Next row K24, turn.

Next row K12, turn.

Work 24 rows in garter st (every row k) on centre 12 sts for instep. Break off yarn.

With right side facing, rejoin yarn at base of instep and pick up and k12 sts along side of instep, k across centre 12 sts then pick up and k12 sts along other side of instep, k rem 12 sts. 60 sts.

K 12 rows. Break off yarn.

Shape Sole

Next row Slip first 24 sts onto right-hand needle, rejoin yarn and k12 sts, turn.

Next row K11, k2tog, turn.

Rep last row until 12 sts rem.

Next row [K2tog] to end.

Cut off yarn, thread through rem sts and fasten off.

Join back seam.

Man's Guernsey-style Sweater

MATERIALS
16(16:18) 50g balls of Debbie Bliss merino double knitting.
Pair each 3¼mm (No 10/US 3) and 4mm (No 8/US 6) knitting needles.

MEASUREMENTS

To fit size	small	medium	large	
Actual chest measurement	105	112	120	cm
	41½	44	47¼	in
Length	66	68	70	cm
	26	26¾	27½	in
Sleeve length	46	48	49	cm
	18	19	19¼	in

TENSION
22 sts and 30 rows to 10cm/4in square over st st on 4mm (No 8/US 6) needles.

ABBREVIATIONS
See page 7.

BACK
With 3¼mm (No 10/US 3) needles cast on 116(124:132) sts.
K 15 rows.
Change to 4mm (No 8/US 6) needles.
Next row K to end.
Next row K4, p to last 4 sts, k4.
Rep last 2 rows 4 times more.
Beg with a k row, cont in st st until back measures 31(32:33)cm/12¼(12½:13)in from beg, ending with a p row.
Inc row (right side) K2,* m1, k1, p2, k1, rep from * to last 2 sts, m1, k2. 145(155:165) sts.
Next row P4, * k2, p3; rep from * to last 6 sts, k2, p4.
Next row K4, * p2, k3; rep from * to last 6 sts, p2, k4.
Rep last 2 rows until work measures 64(66:68) cm/25¼(26:26¾)in from beg, ending with a wrong-side row.
Shape Neck
Next row Rib 56(61:66) sts, turn and work on these sts for first side of neck.
Dec one st at neck edge on next 5 rows. 51(56:61) sts.
Next row K2, k2tog, * p2, k1, k2tog, rep from * to last 2 sts, p2. 41(45:49) sts.
Cast off.
With right side facing, slip centre 33 sts onto a holder, rejoin yarn and patt to end.
Dec one st at neck edge on next 5 rows. 51(56:61) sts.
Next row * P2, k1, k2tog, rep from * to last 6 sts, p2, k1, k1. 41(45:49) sts.

Cast off.

FRONT
Work as given for Back until front measures 58(60:62)cm/22¾(23¾:24½)in from beg, ending with a wrong-side row.
Shape Neck
Next row Rib 61(66:71) sts, turn and work on these sts for first side of neck.
Dec one st at neck edge on next 5 rows and 5 foll alt rows. 51(56:61) sts.
Cont straight until front measures same as Back to shoulder, ending with a wrong-side row.
Next row K2, k2tog, * p2, k1, k2tog, rep from * to last 2 sts, p2. 41(45:49) sts.
Cast off.
With right side facing, slip centre 23 sts onto a holder, rejoin yarn and patt to end.
Dec one st at neck edge on next 5 rows and 5 foll alt rows. 51(56:61) sts.
Cont straight until front measures same as Back to shoulder, ending with a wrong-side row.
Next row * P2, k1, k2tog, rep from * to last 6 sts, p2, k1, k2tog, k1. 41(45:49) sts.
Cast off.

SLEEVES
With 3¼mm (No 10/US 3) needles cast on 54(58:62) sts.
1st row K2, *p2, k2; rep from * to end.
2nd row P2, *k2, p2; rep from * to end.
Rep last 2 rows for 6cm/2½in, ending with a 2nd row.
Change to 4mm (No 8/US 6) needles.
Beg with a k row, work in st st for 4 rows.
Next row K2, m1, k to last 2 sts, m1, k2.
Inc one st at each end of row, as set, on every foll 4th row until there are 88(92:96) sts.
P 1 row.
Inc row K2,* m1, k1, p2, k1, rep from * to last 2 sts, m1, k2. 110(115:120) sts.
Next row [P3, k2] 22(23:24) times.
Next row [P2, k3] 22(23:24) times.
These 2 rows set the rib patt.
Cont in rib patt, inc one one st at each end of the 2nd and every foll 4th row until there are 136(141:146) sts.
Cont straight until sleeve measures 46(48:49)cm/18(19:19¼)in from beg, ending with a wrong-side row.
Cast off in rib.

NECKBAND
Join right shoulder seam.
With 3¼mm (No 10/US 3) needles and right side facing, pick up and k26 sts down left side of front neck, k1, k2tog, [p2, k1, k2tog] 4 times across sts on front neck holder, pick up and k25 sts up right side of front neck, k5 sts down right side of back neck, k1,

k2tog, [p2, k1, k2tog] 6 times across sts on back neck holder, pick up and k6 sts up left side of back neck. 106 sts.
Next row P2, * k2, p2; rep from * to end.
Next row K2, * p2, k2; rep from * to end.
Rep last 2 rows for 8cm/3in then change to 4mm(No 8/US 6) needles and work a further 10cm/4in in rib.
Cast off loosely in rib.

TO MAKE UP

Join left shoulder and neckband seam, reversing seam on last 10cm/4in. Sew on sleeves. Join side and sleeve seams, leaving garter st edging free.

Mohair Cushion

MATERIALS
Two 50g balls of Novita Mohair.
Pair of 4mm (No 8/US 6) knitting needles.
40cm x 40cm/15¾in x 15¾in cushion pad.

MEASUREMENTS
Cushion cover measures 40cm x 40cm/15¾in x 15¾in.

TENSION
20 sts and 28 rows to 10cm/4in square over st st on 4mm
(No 8/US 6) needles.

ABBREVIATIONS
See page 7.

TO MAKE
Using 4mm (No 8/US 6) needles cast on 90 sts.
Cont in st st until piece measures 100cm/39¼in from beg.
Cast off.

TO MAKE UP
Leaving last 20cm/8in free, with right sides together, join side
seams. Turn to right side, fold last 20cm/8in to inside.

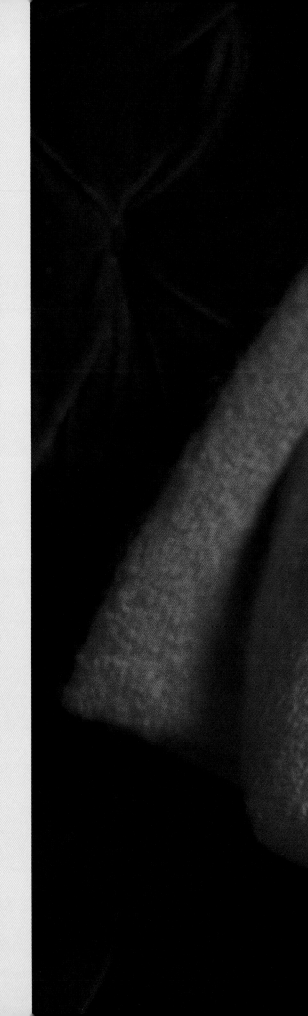

Mohair Throw

MATERIALS
Six 50g balls of Novita Mohair.
Pair of 4mm (No 8/US 6) knitting needles.
4.6m/5yd of 5cm/2in wide satin ribbon if required.

MEASUREMENTS
Throw measures approximately 80cm x 145cm/31½in x 57in
(excluding edging).

TENSION
20 sts and 28 rows to 10cm/4in square over st st on 4mm
(No 8/US 6) needles.

ABBREVIATIONS
See page 7.

MAIN PART
With 4mm (No 8/US 6) needles cast on 160 sts.
1st row * K1, p1; rep from * to end.
2nd row * P1, k1; rep from * to end.
Rep last 2 rows twice more.
Next row Moss st 4, k to last 4 sts, moss st 4.
Next row Moss st 4, p to last 4 sts, moss st 4.
Rep last 2 rows until work measures 143cm/56¼in from beg,
ending with a wrong-side row.
1st row * K1, p1; rep from * to end.
2nd row * P1, k1; rep from * to end.
Rep last 2 rows once more and the first row again.
Cast off in patt.

TO COMPLETE
If you would like to make your throw more deocorative cover moss
st border with ribbon as folls: with right side facing, hand stitch the
edge of the ribbon to the inner edge of the moss st border, **at the
same time** mitre the ribbon to fit the corners of throw. Fold the
ribbon over the edge and stitch the opposite edge of the ribbon to
the inner edge of the moss st border on the wrong side of the
throw.

Moss Stitch Top

MATERIALS
13(14:15) 50g balls of Debbie Bliss wool/cotton.
Pair of 3¼mm (No 10/US 3) knitting needles.
Short 3¼mm (No 10/US 3) circular needle.

MEASUREMENTS

To fit	82	87	92	cm
	32	34	36	in
Actual bust measurement:	88	94	102	cm
	34¾	37	40	in
Length	50.5	53.5	56.5	cm
	19¾	21	22¼	in
Sleeve length	38	40	42	cm
	15	15¾	16½	in

TENSION
25 sts and 40 rows to 10cm/4in square over moss st on 3¼mm
(No 10/US 3) needles.

ABBREVIATIONS
See page 7.

BACK
With 3¼mm (No 10/US 3) needles cast on 113(119:129) sts.
1st row (right side) K1, * p1, k1; rep from * to end.
This row forms the moss st patt.
Moss st 15(17:19) rows.
Dec one st at each end of the next and every foll 6th row until
101(107:119) sts rem.
Work straight until back measures 15(16:17)cm/6(6¼:6¾)in from
beg, ending with a right side row.
Inc one st at each end of the next and every foll 6th row until there
are 101(107:119) sts.
Work straight until back measures 32(34:36)cm/12½(13½:14¼)in
from beg, ending with a wrong-side row.
Shape Armholes
Cast off 5(6:7) sts at beg of next 2 rows.
Dec one st at each end of next and every foll alt row until 83(87:91) sts rem.
Work straight until back measures 50(53:56)cm/19¾(21:22)in from
beg, ending with a wrong-side row.
Shape Back Neck
Next row Patt 32(34:35) sts, turn and work on these sts for first
side of neck shaping.
Next row Cast off 4 sts, patt to end.
Shape Shoulder
Next row Cast off 9 sts, patt to end.
Next row Cast off 2 sts, patt to end.
Next row Cast off 9(10:10) sts, patt to end.
Next row Patt to end.
Next row Cast off rem 8(9:10) sts.

With right side facing, rejoin yarn to rem sts, cast off 19(19:21) sts, patt to end.
Complete to match first side.

FRONT
Work as given for Back until front measures 37(39:41)cm/14½
(15¼:16)in from beg, ending with a wrong-side row.
Front Opening
Next row Moss st 50(53:59), turn and work on these sts for first side of neck.
Work 21 rows.
Shape Neck
Next row Patt to last 8 sts, leave these sts on a holder.
Dec one st at neck edge on every row until 26(28:29) sts rem.
Work straight until front measures same as Back to shoulder,
ending at armhole edge.
Shape Shoulder
Next row Cast off 9 sts, patt to end.
Next row Patt to end.
Next row Cast off 9(10:10) sts, patt to end.
Next row Patt to end.
Next row Cast off rem 8(9:10) sts.
With right side facing, rejoin yarn to rem sts, cast off one st, patt to end.
Complete to match first side.

SLEEVES
With 3¼mm (No 10/US 3) needles cast on 49(53:55) sts.
Moss st 10 rows as given for Back.
Cont in moss st **at the same time** inc and work into patt one st at
each end of the next and every foll 7th row until there are 85(91:97) sts.
Cont straight until sleeve measures 38(40:42)cm/15(15¾:16½)in
from beg, ending with a wrong-side row.
Shape Sleeve Top
Cast off 5(6:7) sts at beg of next 2 rows.
Dec one st at each end of every foll alt row until 57(59:61) sts rem.
Work 3 rows.
Dec one st at each end of the next and every foll 6th row until
51(53:55) sts rem, then on every foll alt row until 45(45:47) sts rem.
Dec one st at each end of the next 4 rows.
Cast off 4 sts at beg of next 2 rows.
Cast off rem 29(29:31) sts.

NECKBAND
Join shoulder seams.
With 3¼mm (No 10/US 3) circular needle and right side facing, pick
up and k15 sts along straight front edge, k8 sts from holder, pick up
and k15 sts to shoulder, 6 sts down right back, 19(19:21) sts
across back neck, 6 sts up left back neck, 15 sts down left front
neck, 8 sts from front neck holder, pick up and k15 sts along
straight front edge. 107(107:109) sts.
K 1 row.
Cast off.

TO MAKE UP
Join side and sleeve seams. Sew in sleeves.

Raglan Sweater

MATERIALS

11(12:13) 50g balls of Debbie Bliss merino aran.
Pair of 5mm (No 6/US 8) knitting needles.
Cable needle.

MEASUREMENTS

To fit	82	87	92	cm
	32	34	36	in
Actual bust measurement	88	94	102	cm
	34¾	37	40	in
Length	61	63	66	cm
	24	25	26	in
Sleeve length	43	44	45	cm
	17	17¼	17¾	in

TENSION

18 sts and 24 rows to 10cm/4in square over st st on 5mm
(No 6/US 8) needles.

ABBREVIATIONS

C4F = slip next 2 sts onto cable needle, hold at front, k2, k2 from
cable needle.
C4B = slip next 2 sts onto cable needle, hold at back, k2, k2 from
cable needle.
See also page 7.

BACK and FRONT (both alike)

With 5mm (No 6/US 8) needles cast on 84(89:96) sts.
Beg with a k row, work 10 rows in st st.
Dec row K3, skpo, k to last 5 sts, k2tog, k3.
Beg with a p row, work 11 rows in st st.
Rep last 12 rows once more and the dec row again. 78(83:90) sts.
Beg with a p row, work 15 rows in st st.

Inc row K3, m1, k to last 3 sts, m1, k3.
Rep last 16 rows once more. 82(87:94) sts.
Beg with a p row, cont in st st until work measures
37(37:38)cm/14½(14½:15)in from beg, ending with a p row.
Shape Raglan Armholes
Cast off 3(3:4) sts at beg of next 2 rows.
1st row K3, skpo, C4F, k to last 9 sts, C4B, k2tog, k3.
2nd row P to end.
3rd row K3, skpo, k to last 5 sts, k2tog, k3.
4th row P to end.
Rep last 4 rows until 30(31:32) sts rem, ending with a p row.
Beg with a k row, work 12 rows st st.
Cast off.

SLEEVES

With 5mm (No 6/US 8) needles cast on 44(47:52) sts.
Beg with a k row, work 10 rows in st st.
Inc row K3, m1, k to last 3 sts, m1, k3.
Beg with a p row, work 7 rows in st st.
Rep last 8 rows until there are 68(73:80) sts.
Cont straight until sleeve measures 43(44:45)cm/17(17¼:17¾)in
from beg, ending with a p row.
Shape Raglan Top
Cast off 3(3:4) sts at beg of next 2 rows.
1st row K3, skpo, C4F, k to last 9 sts, C4B, k2tog, k3.
2nd row P to end.
3rd row K3, skpo, k to last 5 sts, k2tog, k3.
4th row P to end.
Rep last 4 rows until 16(17:18) sts rem, ending with a p row.
Beg with a k row, work 12 rows st st.
Cast off.

TO MAKE UP

Join raglan seams. Join side and sleeve seams. Press edges flat
to prevent rolling.

Ribbed Sweater

MATERIALS
8(10) 50g balls of Debbie Bliss merino double knitting in Main Colour (M).
1(2) balls of same in Contrast Colour (C).
Pair each of 3¼mm (No 10/US 3) and 4mm (No 8/US 6) knitting needles.

MEASUREMENTS

To fit age	2-4	4-6	years
Actual chest measurements	80	88	cm
	31½	34½	in
Length	40	45	cm
	15¾	17¾	in
Sleeve length	25	31	cm
	10	12¼	in

TENSION
36 sts and 30 rows to 10cm/4in square over rib patt (slightly stretched) on 4mm (No 8/US 6) needles.

ABBREVIATIONS
See page 7.

BACK
With 3¼mm (No 10/US 3) needles and C, cast on 146(162) sts.
1st row (right side) K2, * p2, k2; rep from * to end.

2nd row P2, * k2, p2; rep from * to end.
These 2 rows form rib patt.
Cont in patt until back measures 4(5)cm/1½(2)in from beg, ending with a wrong-side row.
Change to 4mm (No 8/US 6) needles and M.
Cont in patt until back measures 40(45)cm/15¾(17¾)in from beg, ending with a wrong-side row.
Shape Shoulders
Cast off 24(27) sts at beg of next 4 rows.
Leave rem 50(54) sts on a holder.

FRONT
Work as given for Back until front measures 35(39)cm/13¾(15¼)in from beg, ending with a wrong-side row.
Shape Neck
Next row Patt 58(64), turn and work on these sts for first side of neck.
Dec one st at neck edge on every row until 48(54) sts rem.
Work straight until front matches Back to shoulder shaping, ending at armhole edge.
Shape Shoulder
Cast off 24(27) sts at beg of next row.
Work 1 row.
Cast off rem 24(27) sts.
With right side facing, slip centre 30(34) sts onto a holder, rejoin yarn to rem sts, patt to end.
Complete to match first side.

SLEEVES
With 3¼mm (No 10/US 3) needles and C, cast on 66(70) sts.
Work 4(5)cm/1½(2)in in rib as given for Back, ending with a wrong-side row.
Change to 4mm (No 8/US 6) needles and M.
Cont in patt, inc one st at each end of every alt row until there are 96(84) sts, then on every foll 3rd row until there are 108(116) sts.
Cont straight until sleeve measures 25(31)cm/10(12¼)in from beg, ending with a wrong-side row.
Cast off.

NECKBAND
Join right shoulder.
With 3¼mm (No 10/US 3) needles and M and with right side facing, pick up and k18 sts down left side of front neck, rib across sts on front neck holder, pick up and k16(20) sts up right side of front neck, then rib back neck sts. 114(126) sts.
Cont in rib across all sts for 12cm/4¾in.
Cast off loosely in rib.

TO MAKE UP
Join left shoulder seam and neckband, reversing seam on last 6cm/2¼in. Sew on sleeves, placing centre of sleeves to shoulder seam. Join side and sleeve seams.

Shirt-style Cardigan

MATERIALS
12(13:14) 50g balls of Debbie Bliss wool/cotton.
Pair each of 3mm (No 11/US 2) and 3¼mm (No 10/US 3) knitting needles.
8 buttons.

MEASUREMENTS

To fit bust	82	87-92	97-102cm
	32	34-36	38-40in
Actual bust measurement	92	102	112 cm
	36	40	44 in
Length	56	58	60 cm
	22	23	23¾ in
Sleeve length	42	44	46 cm
(with cuff turned back)	16½	17¼	18 in

TENSION
25 sts and 34 rows to 10cm/4in square over st st on 3¼mm (No 10/US 3) needles.

ABBREVIATIONS
dec 2tog = slip next 2 sts off needle tog, as if to k them tog, k next st, then pass 2 slipped sts over the knit st and off the needle. See also page 7.

RIGHT BACK
With 3mm (No 11/US 2) needles cast on 61(67:73) sts.
Moss st row K1, * p1, k1; rep from * to end.
Rep last row 6 times more.
Change to 3¼mm (No 10/US 3) needles.
1st row (right side) K to last 4 sts, [p1, k1] twice.
2nd row [K1, p1] twice, k1, p to end.
These 2 rows set the st st with moss st border.
Rep last 2 rows 17 times more.
37th row Patt to last 5 sts, cast off these 5 sts.
Leave rem 56(62:68) sts on a needle.

LEFT BACK
With 3mm (No 11/US 2) needles cast on 61(67:73) sts.
Moss st row K1, * p1, k1; rep from * to end.
Rep last row 6 times more.
Change to 3¼mm (No 10/US 3) needles.
1st row (right side) [K1, p1] twice, k to end.
2nd row P to last 5 sts, k1, [p1, k1] twice.
These 2 rows set the st st with moss st border.
Rep last 2 rows 17 times more, then 1st row again.
38th row P to end, then p across sts of Right Back. 117(129:141) sts.
1st dec row K28(31:34), dec 2tog, k55(61:67), dec 2tog,

k28(31:34). 113(125:137) sts.
St st 3 rows straight.
2nd dec row K27(30:33), dec 2tog, k53(59:65), dec 2tog, k27(30:33). 109(121:133) sts.
St st 3 rows straight.
Cont to dec in this way on the next and every foll 4th row until 85(97:109) sts rem.
St st 3(5:7) rows straight.
1st inc row K21(24:27), m1, k1, m1, k41(47:53), m1, k1, m1, k21(24:27). 89(101:113) sts.
St st 3 rows straight.
2nd inc row K22(25:28), m1, k1, m1, k43(49:55), m1, k1, m1, k22(25:28). 93(105:117) sts.
St st 3 rows straight.
Cont to inc in this way on the next and every foll 4th row until there are 117(129:141) sts.
Cont straight until back measures 36(37:38)cm/14¼(14½:15)in from beg, ending with a wrong-side row.

Shape Armholes
Cast off 6(7:8) sts at beg of next 2 rows.
Dec one st at each end of next and every foll alt row until 93(99:105) sts rem.
Cont straight until back measures 56(58:60)cm/22(23:23¾)in from beg, ending with a wrong-side row.

Shape Shoulders
Cast off 10(11:11) sts at beg of next 4 rows and 9(9:11) sts at beg of foll 2 rows.
Cast off rem 35(37:39) sts.

LEFT FRONT
With 3mm (No 11/US 2) needles cast on 61(67:73) sts.
Moss st row K1, * p1, k1; rep from * to end.
Rep last row 6 times more.
Change to 3¼mm (No 10/US 3) needles.
1st row (right side) K to last 4 sts, [p1, k1] twice.
2nd row [K1, p1] twice, k1, p to end.
These 2 rows set the st st with moss st border.
Work a further 36 rows.
1st dec row K28(31:34), dec 2tog, k26(29:32), [p1, k1] twice. 59(65:71) sts.
Work 3 rows straight.
2nd dec row K27(30:33), dec 2tog, k25(28:31), [p1, k1] twice. 57(63:69) sts.
Work 3 rows straight.
Cont to dec in this way on the next and every foll 4th row until 45(51:57) sts rem.
Work 3(5:7) rows straight.
1st inc row K21(24:27), m1, k1, m1, k19(22:25), [p1, k1] twice. 47(53:59) sts.
Work 3 rows straight.
2nd inc row K22(25:28), m1, k1, m1, k20(23:26), [p1, k1] twice. 49(55:61) sts.

Work 3 rows straight.

Cont to inc in this way on the next and every foll 4th row until there are 61(67:73) sts.

Cont straight until front measures 36(37:38)cm/14¼(14½:15)in from beg, ending with a wrong-side row.

Shape Armhole

Cast off 6(7:8) sts at beg of next row.

Work 1 row.

Dec one st at beg of next and every foll alt row until 49(52:55) sts rem.

Cont straight until front measures 51(52:53)cm/20(20½:21)in from beg, ending with a right-side row.

Shape Neck

Cast off 4 sts at beg of next and foll alt row.

Dec one st at neck edge on every row until 29(31:33) sts rem.

Work straight until front measures same as Back to shoulder, ending at armhole edge.

Shape Shoulder

Cast off 10(11:11) sts at beg of next and foll alt row.

Work 1 row

Cast off rem 9(9:11) sts.

RIGHT FRONT

Mark position for buttons: the 1st 2cm/¾in from beg, the 8th 1cm/½in from beg of neck shaping, and the rem 6 spaced evenly between.

Work buttonholes to match markers as folls:

Buttonhole row (right side) K1, p1, k2tog, yf, k1, patt to end.

With 3mm (No 11/US 2) needles cast on 61(67:73) sts.

Moss st row K1, * p1, k1; rep from * to end.

Rep the last row 6 times more.

Change to 3¼mm (No 10/US 3) needles.

1st row (right side) [K1, p1] twice, k to end.

2nd row P to last 5 sts, k1, [p1, k1] twice.

These 2 rows set the st st with moss st border.

Work a further 36 rows.

1st dec row [K1, p1] twice, k26(29:32), dec 2tog, k28(31:34). 59(65:71) sts.

Work 3 rows straight.

2nd dec row [K1, p1] twice, k25(28:31), dec 2tog, k27(30:33). 57(63:69) sts.

Work 3 rows straight.

Complete to match left front, reversing all shapings.

SLEEVES

Cuffs

First Half With 3mm (No 11/US 2) needles cast on 25(27:29) sts.

Moss st row K1, * p1, k1; rep from * to end.

Rep last row 24 times more.

Leave these sts on a spare needle.

Second Half With 3mm (No 11/US 2) needles cast on 25(27:29) sts.

Moss st row K1, * p1, k1; rep from * to end.

Rep last row 24 times more.

Next row Moss st 24(26:28), work last st of second half tog with first st of first half, moss st 24(26:28). 49(53:57) sts.

Work a further 23 rows in moss st.

Change to 3¼mm (No 10/US 3) needles.

Cont in st st, inc one st at each end of the next and every foll 7th row until there are 81(87:93) sts.

Cont straight until sleeve measures 47(49:51)cm/18½(19¼:20)in from beg, ending with a wrong-side row.

Shape Sleeve Top

Cast off 6(7:8) sts at beg of next 2 rows.

Dec one st at each end of next 3 rows and every foll alt row until 47(49:51) sts rem.

Now dec one st each end of every foll 4th row until 35 sts rem.

Work 1 row.

Dec one st at each end of next and 2 foll alt rows.

Dec one st at each end of next 5 rows.

Cast off 3 sts at beg of next 2 rows. 13 sts.

Cast off.

COLLAR

With 3mm (No 11/US 2) needles cast on 33(37:41) sts.

Moss st row K1, * p1, k1; rep from * to end.

Working in moss st, cast on 10 sts at beg of next 4 rows.

Next row Cast on 10 sts, k1, p2, k1, [k1, p1] 3 times across these sts, then moss st to end.

Next row Cast on 10 sts, k3, p1, [k1, p1] 3 times across these sts, moss st to last 4 sts, p1, k3. 93(97:101) sts.

Work in patt as folls:

1st row K1, p2, k2, * p1, k1; rep from * to last 4 sts, k1, p2, k1.

2nd row (inc row) K3, p1, m1, moss st to last 4 sts, m1, p1, k3.

3rd row K1, p2, k1, moss st to last 4 sts, k1, p2, k1.

4th row K3, p1, moss st to last 4 sts, p1, k3.

5th row (inc row) K1, p2, k1, m1, moss st to last 4 sts, m1, k1, p2, k1.

6th row As 4th row.

7th row As 3rd row.

Rep 2nd to 7th rows twice more, then 2nd and 3rd rows again.

Cast off in patt.

TO MAKE UP

Join shoulder seams. Sew in sleeves. Join side and sleeve seams reversing seam on halves of cuff to fold back. Sew on buttons. Sew cast-off sts on back vent to wrong side. Sew cast-on edge of collar to neck edge, placing edges of collar halfway across front bands. Secure cuff turn backs on sleeve seam.

Simple Top and Socks with Contrast Stripe

MATERIALS
Top 4(5:5) 50g balls of Debbie Bliss wool/cotton in Main Colour (M) and small amount of same in Contrast Colour (C).
Socks One 50g ball of Debbie Bliss wool/cotton in Main Colour (M) and small amount of same in Contrast Colour (C).
Pair each of 2¾mm (No 12/US 2) and 3¼mm (No 10/US 3) knitting needles.
2 buttons.

MEASUREMENTS
Top

To fit ages	3-6	6-12	12-18	months
Actual chest measurement	51	56	62	cm
	20	22	24½	in
Length	25	30	35	cm
	10	12	13¾	in
Sleeve length	15	18	22	cm
	6	7	8¾	in

Socks

To fit	3	6	months

TENSION
25 sts and 34 rows to 10cm/4in square over st st on 3¼mm (No 10/US 3) needles.

ABBREVIATIONS
See page 7.

Top
BACK
With 2¾mm (No 12/US 2) needles and C, cast on 66(72:80) sts.
Rib row * K1, p1; rep from * to end.
Rep last row once more.
Cut off C.
Join on M.
Rib a further 6(8:10) rows.
Change to 3¼mm (No 10/US 3) needles.
Beg with a k row, cont in st st until back measures 25(30:35)cm/10(12:13¾)in from beg, ending with a p row.
Shape Shoulders
Cast off 9(10:11) sts at beg of next 4 rows.
Cast off rem 30(32:36) sts.

FRONT
Work as given for Back until front measures 17(20:23)cm/6¾(8:9)in from beg, ending with a p row.
Front Opening
Next row K30(33:37), turn and work on these sts for first side of neck.
Work straight for 4(5:6)cm/1½(2:2½) in, ending at side edge.
Shape Neck
Next row K to last 5(6:7) sts, leave these sts on a safety pin.
Dec one st at neck edge on every row until 18(20:22) sts rem.
Work straight until front measures same as Back to shoulder, ending at side edge.
Shape Shoulder
Cast off 9(10:11) sts at beg of next row.
Work 1 row.
Cast off rem 9(10:11) sts.
With right side facing, cast off centre 6 sts, k to end.
Complete to match first side.

SLEEVES
Using 2¾mm (No 12/US 2) needles and C, cast on 36(40:44) sts.
Work 2 rows rib as given for Back.
Cut off C.
Join on M.
Rib a further 6(8:10) rows.
Change to 3¼mm (No 10/US 3) needles.
Beg with a k row, cont in st st inc one st at each end of every 3rd row until there are 58(66:74) sts.
Cont straight until sleeve measures 15(18:22)cm/6(7:8¾)in from beg, ending with a p row. Cast off.

BUTTON BAND
Using 2¾mm (No 12/US 2) needles and M, pick up and k15(17:19) sts down left side of front neck opening.
Work 7 rows k1, p1 rib. Cast off.

BUTTONHOLE BAND
Using 2¾mm (No 12/US 2) needles and M, pick up and k15(17:19) sts up right side of front neck opening.
Work 3 rows k1, p1 rib.
Buttonhole row Rib 2, yf, rib 2tog, rib 7(9:11), rib 2tog, yf, rib 2.
Work 3 rows rib.
Cast off.

COLLAR
Join shoulder seams.
With right side facing and using 2¾mm (No 12/US 2) needles and M, pick up and k3 sts from second half of buttonhole band, k5(6:7) sts from safety pin, pick up and k16(18:20) sts up right side of front neck, k30(32:36) sts from back neck, pick up and k17(19:21) sts down left side of front neck, 5(6:7) sts from safety pin, k3 sts from first half of button band. 79(87:97) sts.
Next 2 rows Rib to last 20(24:28) sts, turn.
Next 2 rows Rib to last 16(20:24) sts, turn.
Next 2 rows Rib to last 12(16:20) sts, turn.
Cont in this way, working 4 more sts at end of every row, work 2(4:6) rows.
Next row Rib to end.

Rib a further 8(10:12) rows.
Cut off M.
Join on C.
Rib a further 2 rows.
Cast off in rib.

TO MAKE UP
Sew on sleeves, placing centre of sleeves to shoulder. Join side and sleeve seams. Lap buttonhole band over button band and catch in place. Sew on buttons.

Socks (make 2)
TO MAKE
With 3¼mm (No 10/US 3) needles and C, cast on 36(40) sts.
Rib row * K1, p1; rep from * to end.
Cut off C.
Join on M.
Rib a further 6(8) rows.
Beg with a k row, cont in st st.
Work 2(4) rows.
Dec row K5, k2tog, k to last 7 sts, skpo, k5.
Work 5(7) rows.
Dec row K4, k2tog, k to last 6 sts, skpo, k4.
Work 1(3) rows.
Dec row K3, [k2tog, k6(7)] 3 times, k2tog, k3(4). 28(32) sts.
Shape Heel
Next row P8(9) sts only, turn.
Work 9 rows in st st on these 8(9) sts only.
Dec row P2(3), p2tog, p1, turn.
Next row Sl 1, k3(4).
Dec row P3(4), p2tog, p1, turn.
Next row Sl 1, k4(5).
Dec row P4(5), p2tog.
Leave rem 5(6) sts on a holder.
With wrong side facing, slip centre 12(14) sts onto a holder, rejoin yarn to rem 8(9) sts, p to end.

Work 8 rows in st st on these 8(9) sts.
Dec row K2(3), k2tog tbl, k1, turn.
Next row Sl 1, p3(4).
Dec row K3(4), k2tog tbl, k1, turn.
Next row Sl 1, p4(5).
Dec row K4(5), k2tog tbl, turn.
Next row Sl 1, p4(5).
Shape Instep
Next row K5(6), pick up and k8 sts evenly along inside edge of heel, k12(14) sts from holder, pick up and k8 sts along inside edge of heel and k5(6) sts from holder. 38(42) sts.
P 1 row.
Dec row K11(12), k2tog, k12(14), k2tog tbl, k11(12).
P 1 row.
Dec row K10(11), k2tog, k12(14), k2tog tbl, k10(11).
P 1 row.
Dec row K9(10), k2tog, k12(14), k2tog tbl, k9(10).
P 1 row.
Dec row K8(9), k2tog, k12(14), k2tog tbl, k8(9). 30(34) sts.
Work 13(17) rows straight.
Shape Toe
Dec row K1, [k2tog tbl, k5(6)] 4 times, k1.
P 1 row.
Dec row K1, [k2tog tbl, k4(5)] 4 times, k1.
P 1 row.
Cut off M.
Join on C.
Dec row K1, [k2tog tbl, k3(4)] 4 times, k1.
P 1 row.
Dec row K1, [k2tog tbl, k2(3)] 4 times, k1.
2nd size only
P 1 row.
Dec row K1, [k2tog tbl, k2] 4 times, k1.
Both sizes
Dec row [P2tog tbl] 7 times.
Break off yarn, thread through rem sts and fasten off. Join seam.

Stocking Stitch Sweater

MATERIALS
8(9:10) 50g balls of Debbie Bliss merino aran.
Pair of 5mm (No 6/US 8) knitting needles.

MEASUREMENTS

To fit ages	2	4	6	years
Actual chest measurement	71	80	90	cm
	28	31½	35½	in
Length	35	38	42	cm
	13¾	15	16½	in
Sleeve length	22	25	28	cm
	8¾	10	11	in

TENSION
18 sts and 24 rows to 10cm/4in square over st st on 5mm
(No 6/US 8) needles.

ABBREVIATIONS
See page 7.

BACK
With 5mm (No 6/US 8) needles cast on 66(74:82) sts.
1st row K2, * p2, k2; rep from * to end.
2nd row P2, * k2, p2; rep from * to end.
Rep last 2 rows 3(4:5) times more.
Beg with a k row, work in st st until back measures
20(22:24)cm/8(8¾:9½)in from beg, ending with a p row.
Shape Raglan Armholes
Cast off 5(6:7) sts at beg of next 2 rows.
1st row K3, skpo, k to last 5 sts, k2tog, k3.

2nd row P3, p2tog, p to last 5 sts, p2togtbl, p3.
3rd–5th rows Rep 1st and 2nd rows, then 1st row again.
6th row P to end.
Rep 5th–6th rows until 20(22:24) sts rem, ending with a p row.
Leave sts on a holder

POCKET LININGS (make 2)
With 5mm (No 6/US 8) needles cast on 18(22:26) sts.
Beg with a k row work 19(21:23) rows in st st, ending with a k row.

FRONT
With 5mm (No 6/US 8) needles cast on 66(74:82) sts.
1st row K2, * p2, k2; rep from * to end.
2nd row P2, * k2, p2; rep from * to end.
Rep last 2 rows 3(4:5) times more.
Beg with a k row, work 18(20:22) rows in st st, ending with a p
row.
Place Pocket
Next row K7 sts, k next 18(22:26) sts and leave these sts on a
holder, k16, k next 18(22:26) sts and leave these sts on a holder,
k last 7 sts.
Next row P7 sts, p across 18(22:26) sts of one pocket lining,
p16, p across 18(22:26) sts of second pocket lining, p7.
Cont in st st until front measures 20(22:24)cm/8(8¾:9½)in from
beg, ending with a p row.
Shape Raglan Armholes
Cast off 5(6:7) sts at beg of next 2 rows.
1st row K3, skpo, k to last 5 sts, k2tog, k3.
2nd row P3, p2tog, p to last 5 sts, p2togtbl, p3.
3rd–5th rows Rep 1st and 2nd rows, then 1st row again.
6th row P to end.
Rep 5th–6th rows until 20(22:24) sts rem, ending with a p row.
Leave sts on a holder.

SLEEVES

With 5mm (No 6/US 8) needles cast on 38(42:46) sts.

1st row K2, * p2, k2; rep from * to end.

2nd row P2, * k2, p2; rep from * to end.

Rep last 2 rows 3(4:5) times more.

Work in st st, inc one st at each end of every foll 3rd and 4th row alternately until there are 60(66:72) sts.

Cont straight until sleeve measures 22(25:28)cm/8¾(10:11)in from beg, ending with a p row.

Shape Raglan Top

Cast off 5(6:7) sts at beg of next 2 rows.

1st row K3, skpo, k to last 5 sts, k2tog, k3.

2nd row P to end.

Rep last 2 rows until 14 sts rem, ending with a p row.

Leave sts on a holder.

COLLAR

With 5mm (No 6/US 8) needles and right side facing, k7, m1, k7 across sts of one sleeve, k across 20(24:28) sts from front neck holder, k7, m1, k7 across sts of second sleeve, k across 20(24:28) sts from from back neck holder. 70(78:86) sts.

Next row K2, * p2, k2; rep from * to end.

Next row P2, * k2, p2; rep from * to end.

Rep last 2 rows until collar measures 10(12:14) cm/4(4¾:5½)in, ending with a wrong-side row.

Cast off loosely in rib.

POCKET TOPS

With 5mm (No 6/US 8) needles and right side facing, work across pocket tops as folls:

1st row K2, * p2, k2; rep from * to end.

2nd row P2, * k2, p2; rep from * to end.

Rep last 2 rows once more.

Cast off in rib.

TO MAKE UP

Join raglan seams. Join side and sleeve seams. Sew down pocket linings and tops.

Woman's Alpaca Wraparound Cardigan

MATERIALS
15(16) 50g balls of Novita Alpaca.
Pair each of 3¼mm (No 10/US 3) and 3¾mm (No 9/US 5) knitting needles.
Long 3¼mm (No 10/US 3) circular knitting needle.

MEASUREMENTS

To fit size	87-92	97-102	cm
	34-36	38-40	in
Actual bust measurement	128	138	cm
	50½	54½	in
Length	62	66	cm
	24½	26	in
Sleeve length	38	40	cm
(with cuff turned back)	15	15¾	in

TENSION
22 sts and 34 rows to 10cm/4in square over st st on 3¾mm (No 9/US 5) needles.

ABBREVIATIONS
See page 7

BACK
With 3¼mm (No 10/US 3) needles cast on 142(154) sts.
1st row K2, * p2, k2; rep from * to end.
2nd row P2, * k2, p2; rep from * to end.
Rep last 2 rows for 4cm/1½in.
Change to 3¾mm (No 9/US 5) needles.
Beg with a k row, cont in st st until work measures 62(66)cm/24½(26)in from beg, ending with a p row.
Shape Shoulders
Cast off 17(18) sts at beg of next 6 rows.
Cast off rem 40(46) sts.

POCKET LININGS (make 2)
With 3¾mm (No 9/US 5) needles cast on 34 sts.
Beg with a k row, cont in st st until work measures 15cm/6in from beg, ending with a p row.
Leave these sts on a holder.

LEFT FRONT
With 3¼mm (No 10/US 3) needles cast on 67(71) sts.
1st row K2, * p2, k2; rep from * to last 5 sts, p2, k3.
2nd row K1, p2, * k2, p2; rep from * to end.
Rep last 2 rows for 4cm/1½in
Change to 3¾mm (No 9/US 5) needles.

Beg with a k row, work in st st until left front measures 15cm/6in from beg, ending with a p row.
Place Pocket
Next row K18(20), slip next 34 sts onto a holder, k across sts on one pocket lining, k15(17).
Cont in st st until work measures 46(49)cm/18(19¼)in from beg, ending with a p row.
Shape Neck
Dec one st at neck edge on every foll alt row until 51(54) sts rem. Work straight until front measures same as Back to shoulder, ending at side edge.
Shape Shoulder
Cast off 17(18) sts at beg of next row and foll alt row.
Work 1 row.
Cast off rem 17(18) sts.

RIGHT FRONT
With 3¼mm (No 10/US 3) needles cast on 65(69) sts.
1st row K2, * p2, k2; rep from * to last 5 sts, p2, k3.
2nd row K1, p2, * k2, p2; rep from * to end.
Rep last 2 rows for 4cm/1½in.
Change to 3¾mm(No 9/US 5) needles.
Beg with a k row, work in st st until right front measures 15cm/6in from beg, ending with a p row.
Place Pocket
Next row K15(17), slip next 34 sts onto a holder, k across sts on second pocket lining, k18(20).
Complete to match Left Front, reversing shapings.

SLEEVES
With 3¾mm (No 9/US 5) needles cast on 62(66) sts.
1st row K2, * p2, k2; rep from * to end.
2nd row P2, * k2, p2; rep from * to end.
Rep last 2 rows for 8cm/3in, ending with a 2nd row.
Change to 3¼mm(No 10/US 3) needles.
Work a further 8cm/3in in rib, ending with a 2nd row.
Change to 3¾mm(No 9/US 5) needles.
Beg with a k row, work in st st, inc one st at each end of the 3rd and every foll 4th row until there are 110(118) sts.
Cont straight until sleeve measures 46(48)cm/18(18¾)in from beg, ending with a p row.
Cast off.

POCKET TOPS
With right side facing and using 3¼mm(No 10/US 3) needles, work 2cm/¾in in k2, p2 rib as given for Back across pocket top.
Cast off in rib.

FRONTBAND AND COLLAR
Join shoulder seams.
With right side facing and using 3¼mm(No 10/US 3) circular needle, pick up and k106(112) sts evenly along straight right front edge to beg of neck shaping, 49(51) sts along shaped edge to

right shoulder, 36(40) sts across back, 49(51) sts along shaped edge to beg of neck shaping, 106(112) sts along straight left front edge to cast-on edge. 346(366) sts.

Work backwards and forwards in rows as follows:

Beg with the 2nd row, work 1 row rib as given for Back.

Shape Collar

1st row Rib 197(209) sts, turn.

2nd row Rib 48(52), turn.

3rd row Rib 54(58), turn.

4th row Rib 60(64), turn.

Cont in this way for a further 16 turning rows, taking an extra 6 sts, as before, on each row.

Next row Rib to end.

Rib 13 rows across all sts.

Cast off in rib.

BELT

With 3¼mm (No 10/US 3) needles cast on 14 sts.

1st row K2, * p2, k2; rep from * to end.

2nd row K1, p1, k2, * p2, k2; rep from * to last 2 sts, p1, k1.

Rep last 2 rows until belt measures 160cm/63in from beg, ending with a 2nd row.

Cast off in rib.

TO MAKE UP

Sew on sleeves. Join side and sleeve seams, reversing seam on cuff for 8cm/3in. Sew down pocket linings and pocket tops. Make a belt carrier at waist level on each side seam.

Hooded Jacket

MATERIALS
10(11:12:13:14) 50g balls of Debbie Bliss merino aran.
Pair each of 5mm (No 6/US 8) and 4½mm (No 7 /US 7)
knitting needles.
6 buttons.

MEASUREMENTS

To fit age	3-4	4-5	6-7	8-9	9-10	years
Actual chest measurement						
	94	100	108	118	128	cm
	37	39½	42½	46½	50½	in
Length	51	56	59	68	71	cm
	20	22	23¼	26¾	28	in
Sleeve length	22	26	30	33	35	cm
(with cuff turned back)	8¾	10¼	11¾	13	13¾	in

TENSION
18 sts and 24 rows to 10cm/4in square over st st on 5mm
(No 6/US 8) needles.

ABBREVIATIONS
See page 7.

BACK
With 5mm (No 6/US 8) needles cast on 87(92:99:108:117) sts.
Beg with a k row, cont in st st until back measures
51(56:59:68:71)cm/20(22:23¼:26¾:28)in from beg, ending with a
p row.
Shape Shoulders
Cast off 31(33:35:39:43) sts at beg of next 2 rows.
Leave rem 25(26:29:30:31) sts on a holder.

POCKET LININGS (make 2)
With 5mm (No 6/US 8) needles cast on 21(23:25:27:29) sts.
Beg with a k row, work 10(12:14:16:18)cm/4(4¾:5½:6¼:7)in in st
st, ending with a k row.

LEFT FRONT
With 5mm (No 6/US 8) needles cast on 45(48:51:56:60) sts.
1st row (right side) K to end.
2nd row K4, p to end.
Rep last 2 rows until front measures 14(16:18:20:22)cm/ 5½
(6¼:7:8:8¾)in from beg, ending with a wrong-side row.
Next row K12(12:13:14:15), cast off 21(23:25:27:29) sts,
k12(13:13:15:16).
Next row K4, p8(9:9:11:12), p across sts of one pocket lining,
p12(12:13:14:15).
Cont straight until front measures 51(56:59:68:71)cm/20
(22:23¼:26¾:28)in from beg, ending with a wrong-side row.

Shape Shoulder

Cast off 31(33:35:39:43) sts at beg of next row.

Next row K4, p to end.

Leave rem 14(15:16:17:17) sts on a holder.

Mark position for buttons: the 1st 13(15:17:19:21)cm/5 (6:6¾:7½:8¼)in from beg, the 6th 4(5:5:6:6)cm/1½(2:2:2½:2½)in from shoulder edge, the rem 4 spaced evenly between.

RIGHT FRONT

With 5mm (No 6/US 8) needles cast on 45(48:51:56:60) sts.

1st row (right side) K to end.

2nd row P to last 4 sts, k4.

Rep last 2 rows until front measures 14(16:18:20:22)cm/5½ (6¼:7:8:8¾)in from beg, ending with a wrong-side row, **at the same time** work buttonholes to match markers as follows:

Buttonhole row (right side) K1, k2tog, yf, k to end.

Next row K12(13:13:15:16), cast off 21(23:25:27:29) sts, k12(12:13:14:15).

Next row P12(12:13:14:15), p across sts of one pocket lining, p8(9:9:11:12), k4.

Cont straight until front measures 51(56:59:68:71)cm/20(22: 23¼:26¾:28)in from beg, ending with a right-side row.

Shape Shoulder

Cast off 31(33:35:39:43) sts at beg of next row.

Leave rem 14(15:16:17:17) sts on a holder.

Do not break off yarn.

SLEEVES

With 5mm (No 6/US 8) needles cast on 50(52:54:56:58) sts.

K 5 rows.

Beg with a k row, cont in st st until sleeve measures 5(6:6:7:7)cm/2(2½:2½:2¾:2¾)in from beg, ending with a p row.

Change to 4mm (No 7/US 7) needles.

Work a further 5(6:6:7:7)cm/2(2½:2 ½:2¾:2¾)in st st.

Change to 5mm (No 6/US 8) needles.

Cont in st st **at the same time** inc one st at each end of the next and every foll 3rd row until there are 74(82:86:90:96) sts.

Work straight until sleeve measures 27(32:36:40:42)cm/10½ (12¾:14¼:15¾:16½)in from beg, ending with a p row.

Cast off.

HOOD

Join shoulder seams.

With 5mm (No 6/US 8) needles and right side facing, k across 14(15:16:17:17) sts from right front holder, k1(2:1:2:1), [m1, k2] 12(12:14:14:15) times across back neck sts, k across 14(15:16:17:17) sts from left front holder. 65(68:75:78:80) sts.

Next row K4, p to last 4 sts, k4.

Next row K to end.

Next row K4, p to last 4 sts, k4.

Inc row K4, m1, k to last 4 sts, m1, k4.

Keeping 4 sts at front edge in garter st (every row k), work 5 rows straight. Rep last 6 rows twice more, then the inc row again. Work 7 rows straight.

Rep last 8 rows 4 times more and the inc row again.

Work 1(3:5:7:9) rows straight.

Cast off.

TO MAKE UP

Join top seam of hood. Sew down pocket linings. Sew on sleeves. Join side and sleeve seams, reversing seam on cuff for 5(6:6:7:7)cm/2(2½:2½:2¾:2¾)in. Sew on buttons.

TENSION

28 sts and 32 rows to 10cm/4in square over rib patt on 3¼mm (No 10/US 3) needles.

ABBREVIATIONS

See page 7.

BACK

With 3¼mm (No 10/US 3) needles and A, cast on 61 sts.
Beg with a k row, work 6 rows st st.
1st rib row K6, * p1, k5; rep from * last 7 sts, p1, k6.
2nd rib row P6, * k1, p5; rep from * last 7 sts, k1, p6.
These 2 rows form the rib patt.
Rep last 2 rows twice more.
Cont in rib and stripe patt as folls:
2 rows C, 2 rows B, 2 rows A, 6 rows B, 2 rows C, 1 row B, 1 row A, 1 row D, 2 rows A, 2 rows D, 2 rows A, 2 rows B, 1 row C, 1 row B, 1 row A, 1 row C, 4 rows B, 1 row D, 2 rows B, 2 rows D, 2 rows B, 1 row D, 4 rows B, 1 row C, 1 row A, 1 row B, 1 row C, 2 rows B, 2 rows A, 1 row B.
Cont in B only.
Shape Top
Next row Patt 19, turn and work on these sts only.
Next row Patt to end.
Dec one st at inner edge on every row until 3 sts rem.
Cast off.
With right side facing, rejoin yarn to rem sts, cast off centre 23 sts, patt to end.
Complete to match first side.

FRONT

Work as given for Back.

EDGINGS (both sides alike)

With right side facing and using 3¼mm (No 10/US 3) needles and B, pick up and k64 sts along shaped edge.
Beg with a p row, work 5 rows st st.
Cast off.

STRAP

With 3¼mm (No 10/US 3) needles and B, cast on 118 sts.
Beg with a k row, work 5 rows in st st.
Cast off.

TO COMPLETE

Leaving edgings free and centre 18cm/7in open, sew top edges together. Sew in zip. Join side and lower edges. Make 3 pompoms in assorted colours and sew to lower edge. Sew on buttons to decorate. Sew ends of strap to top of side seams.

Striped Bag

MATERIALS

One 50g ball each of Debbie Bliss merino double knitting in Red (A), Light Pink (B), Rust (C) and Grey (D).
Pair of 3¼mm (No 10/US 3) knitting needles.
18cm/7in lightweight zip.

MEASUREMENTS

Bag measures 21cm x 25cm/8¼in x 9¾in.

Striped Garter Stitch Jacket

MATERIALS
2(2:2) 50g balls each of Debbie Bliss merino double knitting in
Light Pink (B) and Blue (F).
1(1:1) ball each of same in Brown (A), Red (C), Fuchsia Pink (D)
and Cream (E).
Pair each of 3¼mm (No10/US 3) and 3¾mm (No9/US 5) knitting
needles.
6(6:7) buttons.

MEASUREMENTS

To fit age	6–9	9–12	12–24months	
Actual chest measurement	56	62	70	cm
	22	24½	27½	in
Length	26	30	33	cm
	10¼	11¾	13	in
Sleeve length	16	18	20	cm
(with cuff turned back)	6¼	7	8	in

TENSION
22 sts and 44 rows to 10cm/4in square over garter st (every row k)
on 3¾mm (No9/US 5) needles.

ABBREVIATIONS
See page 7.

BACK AND FRONTS
With 3¾mm (No 9/US 5) needles and A cast on 124(136:154) sts.
K 3 rows.
Cont in stripe patt as folls:
K 4 rows D, 4 rows C, 8 rows B, 2 rows E, 6 rows F and 2 rows
A.
Cont straight in garter st until work measures 15(17:19)cm/6
(6¾:7½)in from beg, ending with a wrong-side row.

Divide for Back and Fronts

Next row K31(34:39), leave these sts on a holder for right front, k next 62(68:76), leave these sts on a holder for back, k to end.

Left Front

Work straight on last set of 31(34:39) sts until front measures 22(25:27)cm/8¾(9¾:10½)in from beg, ending at neck edge.

Shape Neck

Next row K7(8:9) sts, leave these sts on a safety pin, k to end.
Dec one st at neck edge on every row until 15(17:19) sts rem.
Work straight until front measures 26(30:33)cm/10¼(11¾:13)in from beg, ending at armhole edge.

Shape Shoulder

Cast off.

Back

With wrong side facing, rejoin yarn to next st.
Work straight until back measures same as left front to shoulder, ending with a wrong-side row.

Shape Shoulders

Cast off 15(17:19) sts at beg of next 2 rows.
Leave rem 32(34:38) sts on a spare needle.

Right Front

With wrong side facing, rejoin yarn to next st, work to match left front.

SLEEVES

Using 3¾mm (No9/US 5) needles and B cast on 35(38:41) sts.
K 7 rows B, 4 rows C, 4 rows D.
K 5 rows A to reverse stripe patt.
Cont in stripes of 4 rows D, 4 rows C, 8 rows B, 2 rows E, 6 rows F and 2 rows A, **at the same time** inc and work into patt one st at each end of the 15th and every foll 6th row until there are 51(56:63) sts.

Work straight until sleeve measures 20(22:24)cm/8(8¾:9½) from beg, ending with a wrong-side row.
Cast off.

NECKBAND

Join shoulder seams.
With right side facing, using 3¼mm (No10/US 3) needles slip 7(8:9) sts from safety pin, join in A, pick up and k12(14:16) sts up right front neck edge, k across 32(34:38) sts on back neck, pick up and k12(14:16) sts down left side of front neck, k7(8:9) sts from safety pin. 70(78:88) sts.
K 3 rows.
Cast off.

BUTTON BAND

With right side facing, using 3¼mm (No10/US 3) needles and A, pick up and k54(60:66) sts along left front edge.
K 3 rows.
Cast off.

BUTTONHOLE BAND

With right side facing, using 3¼mm (No10/US 3) needles and A, pick up and k54(60:66) sts along right front edge.
K 1 row.
Buttonhole row K1(1:2) sts, [k2tog, yf, k8(9:8) sts] 5(5:6) times, k2tog, yf, k1(2:2).
K 1 row.
Cast off.

TO MAKE UP

Join sleeve seams, reversing seam on cuff for 4cm/1½in. Sew in sleeves. Sew on buttons.

Striped Sweater

MATERIALS

8(8:9:9:10) 50g balls of Debbie Bliss merino aran in Main Colour (M).

1 ball each of same in Red (A), Pink (B), Lime Green (C), Sea Green (D) and Oatmeal (E).

Pair each of 3¾mm (No 9/US 4) and 5mm (No 6/US 8) knitting needles.

MEASUREMENTS

To fit age	2-3	3-4	4-6	6-8	8-9	years
Actual chest measurement	78	84	93	98	105	cm
	30¾	33	36½	38½	41½	in
Length	43	46	49	53	57	cm
	17	18	19¼	21	22½	in
Sleeve length	28	30	32	37	40	cm
	11	11¾	12½	14½	15¾	in

TENSION

18 sts and 24 rows to 10cm/4in square over rib patt on 5mm (No 6/US 8) needles.

ABBREVIATIONS

See page 7.

BACK

With 5mm (No 6/US 8) needles and M, cast on 73(79:85:91:97) sts.

1st row (right side) K6, * p1, k5; rep from * to last 7 sts, p1, k6.

2nd row P to end.

These 2 rows form rib patt.

Work 2 more rows.

Cont in rib and stripe patt as folls:

1 row A, 1 row B, 2 rows M, 1 row C, 1 row D, 1 row E, 2 rows M, 1 row E, 1 row B, 1 row A, 1 row B, 1 row E, 2 rows M, 1 row C, 1 row D, 1 row C, 1 row E, 6 rows M.

These 26 rows form the stripe patt.

Cont in patt until back measures 26(28:30:33:36)cm/10 ¼(11: 11¾:13:14)in from beg, ending with a wrong-side row.

Shape Armholes

Cast off 6 sts at beg of next 2 rows. 61(67:73:79:85) sts.

Cont in patt until back measures 43(46:49:53:57) cm/17(18: 19¼:21:22½) in from beg, ending with a wrong-side row.

Shape Shoulders

Cast off 17(19:21:23:25) sts at beg of next 2 rows.

Cast off rem 27(29:31:33:35) sts.

FRONT

Work as given for Back until front measures 38(40:43:46:50)cm/15(15¾:17:18¼:19¾)in from beg, ending with a wrong-side row.

Shape Neck

Next row Patt 25(28:30:33:35), turn and work on these sts for first side of neck.

Dec one st at neck edge on every row until 17(19:21:23:25) sts rem.

Work straight until front matches Back to shoulder shaping, ending at armhole edge.

Shape Shoulder

Cast off rem 17(19:21:23:25) sts.

With right side facing, rejoin yarn to rem sts, cast off centre 11(11:13:13:15) sts, patt to end.

Complete to match first side.

SLEEVES

With 5mm (No 6/US 8) needles and E, cast on 33(33:35:37:37) sts.

1st row (right side) K1(1:2:3:3), * p1, k5; rep from * to last 2(2:3:4:4) sts, p1, k1(1:2:3:3).

2nd row P to end.

These 2 rows set the rib patt.

Cont in rib and stripe patt as folls **at the same time** inc one st at each end of the 7th and every foll 4th row until there are 61(63:67:73:77) sts:

2 rows M, 1 row E, 1 row C, 1 row D, 1 row C, 2 rows M, 1 row E, 1 row B, 1 row A, 1 row B, 1 row E, then cont in M only.

Cont straight until sleeve measures 28(30:32:37:40)cm/11(11¾: 12½:14½:15¾)in from beg, ending with a wrong-side row.

Mark each end of last row.

Work a further 8 rows.

Cast off.

COLLAR

With 3¾mm (No 9/US 4) needles and M, cast on 30(30:30:34:34) sts.

1st row K2, * p2, k2; rep from * to end.

2nd row P2, * k2, p2; rep from * to end.

3rd row Cast on 4 sts, k2, p2 across these 4 sts, then rib to end.

4th row Cast on 4 sts, p2, k2 across these sts, then rib to end.

Rep last 2 rows 4(4:4:5:5) times more.

Next row Cast on 5 sts, k3, p2 across these 5 sts, then rib to end.

Next row Cast on 5 sts, k1, p2, k2 across these sts, then rib to last st, k1.

Cont in rib as set, work 6(6:6:8:8) rows straight.

Cut off M.

Join on E.

Rib 1 row.

Cast off loosely in rib.

TO MAKE UP

Join shoulder seams. Sew on sleeves, placing centre of sleeves to shoulder seam and last 8 rows to cast-off sts at underarm. Join side and sleeve seams.

Woman's Alpaca Polo Neck

MATERIALS
10(11:12) 50g balls of Novita Alpaca.
Pair each of 3¼mm (No 10/US 3) and 4mm (No 8/US 6) knitting needles.

MEASUREMENTS

To fit size	87	91	96	cm
	32	34	36	in
Actual bust measurement	91	100	110	cm
	35¾	39½	43½	in
Length	51	56	61	cm
	20	22	24	in
Sleeve length	46	47	48	cm
(with cuff turned back)	18	18½	19	in

TENSION
21 sts and 30 rows to 10cm/4in square over st st on 4mm (No 8/US 6) needles.

ABBREVIATIONS
See page 7.

BACK
With 3¼mm (No 10/US 3) needles cast on 86(94:102) sts.
1st row K2, * p2, k2; rep from * to end.
2nd row P2, * k2, p2; rep from * to end.
Rep last 2 rows for 7cm/2¾in
Change to 4mm (No 8/US 6) needles.
Beg with a k row, work in st st for 4(6:8) rows.
Inc row K3, m1, k to last 3 sts, m1, k3.
Inc one st at each end of row, as set, on every foll 10th row until there are 98(108:118) sts.
Cont straight until back measures 32(35:38)cm/12½(14:15)in from beg, ending with a p row.
Shape Armholes
Next row K3, k2tog, k to last 5 sts, sl 1, k1, psso, k3.
Next row P to end.
Rep last 2 rows 7(8:9) times more. 82(90:98) sts.
Work straight until back measures 49(54:59)cm/19¼(21¼:23¼)in from beg, ending with a p row.
Shape Neck
Next row K30(33:36), turn and work on these sts for first side of neck.
Dec one st at neck edge on next 4 rows. 26(29:32) sts.
P 1 row.
Shape Shoulder
Cast off 13(14:16) sts at beg of next row.
Work 1 row.
Cast off rem 13(15:16) sts.
With right side facing, slip centre 22(24:26) sts onto a holder, rejoin yarn to rem sts, k to end.
Complete to match first side.

FRONT
Work as given for Back until front measures 43(48:53)cm/17(19:21)in from beg, ending with a p row.
Shape Neck
Next row K33(36:39), turn and work on these sts for first side of neck.
Dec one st at neck edge on every foll alt row until 26(29:32) sts rem.
Work straight until front matches Back to shoulder shaping, ending at armhole edge.
Shape Shoulder
Cast off 13(14:16) sts at beg of next row.
Work 1 row.
Cast off rem 13(15:16) sts.
With right side facing, slip centre 16(18:20) sts onto a holder, rejoin yarn to rem sts, k to end.
Complete to match first side.

SLEEVES
With 4mm (No 8/US 6) needles cast on 46(50:54) sts.
1st row K2, * p2, k2; rep from * to end.
2nd row P2, * k2, p2; rep from * to end.
Rep last 2 rows for 5cm/2in.
Change to 3¼mm (No 10/US 3) needles.
Work a further 5cm/2in rib.
Change to 4mm (No 8/US 6) needles.
Beg with a k row, work in st st for 4 rows.
Inc row K3, m1, k to last 3 sts, m1, k3.
Inc one st at each end of row, as set, on every foll 6th row until there are 76(82:88) sts.
Work straight until sleeve measures 51(52:53)cm/20(20½:21)in from beg, ending with a wrong-side row.
Shape Sleeve Top
Next row K3, k2tog, k to last 5 sts, sl 1, k1, psso, k3.
Next row P to end.
Rep last 2 rows 7(8:9) times more. 60(64:68) sts.
Cast off.

NECKBAND
Join right shoulder.
With 3¼mm (No 10/US 3) needles and right side facing, pick up and k23 sts down left side of front neck, k16(18:20) sts on front neck holder, pick up and k23 sts up right side of front neck, 9 sts down right side of back neck, k22(24:26) sts on back neck holder, pick up and k9 sts up left side of back neck. 102(106:110) sts.
Next row P2, * k2, p2; rep from * to end.
Next row K2, * p2, k2; rep from * to end.
Rep last 2 rows for 8cm/3in then change to 4mm (No 8/US 6) needles and work a further 10cm/4in in rib.
Cast off loosely in rib.

TO MAKE UP
Join left shoulder seam and neckband, reversing seam on last 12cm/4¾in. Sew on sleeves. Join side and sleeve seams, reversing seam on last 5cm/2in.

Jacket with Fair Isle Border

MATERIALS
6(8) balls of Debbie Bliss merino double knitting in Brown (M).
1(1) ball each of same in Fuchsia Pink, Light Pink, Red, Pale Blue, Stone and Cream.
Pair each of 3¼mm (No 10/US 3) and 4mm (No 8/US 6) knitting needles.
35(40)cm/14(15¾)in open-ended zip.

MEASUREMENTS

To fit age	3-4	4-5	years
Actual chest measurement	81	90	cm
	32	35½	in
Length	40	45	cm
	15¾	17¾	in
Sleeve length	23	27	cm
	9	10¾	in

TENSION
22 sts and 30 rows to 10cm/4cm square over patt on 4mm (No 8/US 6) needles.

ABBREVIATIONS
See page 7.

NOTE
Read chart from right to left on right side rows and from left to right on wrong side rows. When working in pattern, strand yarn not in use loosely across wrong side to keep fabric elastic.

BACK
With 3¼mm (No 10/US 3) needles and M cast on 91(101) sts.
Moss st row K1, * p1, k1; rep from * to end.
Rep this row 5 times more.
Change to 4mm (No 8/US 6) needles.
Beg with a k row, work in st st until back measures 23(26)cm/9(10¼)in from beg, ending with a p row.
Work in patt from Chart until 17 rows of Chart have been worked.
Cont in M and st st until back measures 40(45)cm/15¾(17¾)in from beg, ending with a p row.
Shape Shoulders
Cast off 16(18) sts at beg of next 4 rows.
Cast off rem 27(29) sts.

POCKET LININGS (make 2)
With 4mm (No 8/US 6) needles and M cast on 21 sts.
Beg with a k row, work in st st for 30 rows. Leave sts on a holder.

LEFT FRONT
With 3¼mm (No 10/US 3) needles and M cast on 45(49) sts.

Work 6 rows moss st as given for Back.
Change to 4mm (No 8/US 6) needles.
Next row K to last 4 sts, moss st 4.
Next row Moss st 4, p to end.
Working moss st border at front edge, work a further 25 rows.
Next row Moss st 4, p10(12), [k1, p1] 10 times, k1, p10(12).
Next row K11(13), [p1, k1] 10 times, k10(12), moss st 4.
Rep last 2 rows once more.
Place Pocket
Next row Moss st 4, p10(12), cast off 21 sts in moss st, p to end.
Next row K10(12), k across pocket lining, k to last 4 sts, moss st 4.
Cont in st st with moss st border until front measures 23(26)cm/9(10¼)in from beg, ending with a wrong-side row.
Next row Work in patt from Chart to last 4 sts, moss st 4 in M.
Next row Moss st 4 in M, work in patt from Chart to end.
Work as set until 17 rows of Chart have been worked.
Cont in M as before until front measures 36(41)cm/14¼(16¼)in from beg, ending with a wrong-side row.
Shape Neck
Next row K to last 6 sts, k2tog, turn, leaving rem 4 sts on a safety pin
Dec one st at neck edge on every row until 32(36) sts rem.
Cont without further shaping until front measures same as Back to shoulder, ending at side edge.
Shape Shoulder
Cast off 16(18) sts at beg of next row. Work 1 row.
Cast off rem 16(18) sts.

RIGHT FRONT
With 3¼mm (No 10/US 3) needles and M cast on 45(49) sts.
Work 6 rows moss st as given for Back.
Change to 4mm (No 8/US 6) needles.
Next row Moss st 4, k to end.
Next row P to last 4 sts, moss st 4.
Working moss st border at front edge, work a further 25 rows.
Next row P10(12), k1, [p1, k1] 10 times, p10(12), moss st 4.
Next row Moss st 4, k10(12), [k1, p1] 10 times, k11(13).
Rep last 2 rows once more.
Place Pocket
Next row P10(12), cast off 21 sts in moss st, p10(12), moss st 4.
Next row Moss st 4, k10(12), k across pocket lining, k to last 4 sts, moss st 4.
Cont in st st with moss st border until front measures 23(26)cm/9(10¼)in from beg, ending with a wrong-side row.
Next row Work in patt from Chart to last 4 sts, moss st 4 in M.
Next row Moss st 4 in M, work in patt from Chart to end.
Work as set until 17 rows of Chart have been worked.
Cont in M as before until front measures 36(41)cm/14¼(16¼)in from beg, ending with a wrong-side row.
Shape Neck
Next row Moss st 4, leave these sts on a safety pin, k2tog, k to end.
Dec one st at neck edge on every row until 32(36) sts rem.
Cont without further shaping until front measures same as Back to

shoulder, ending at side edge.
Shape Shoulder
Cast off 16(18) sts at beg of next row.
Patt 1 row.
Cast off rem 16(18) sts.

SLEEVES
With 3¼mm (No 10/US 3) needles and M cast on 33(37) sts.
Work 6 rows moss st as given for Back.
Change to 4mm (No 8/US 6) needles.
Working in st st, inc one st at each end of 3rd and every foll 4th row until there are 61(69) sts.
Cont straight until sleeve measures 23(27)cm/9(10¾)in from beg, ending with a p row.
Cast off.

RIGHT COLLAR
Join shoulder seams.
With right side facing, using 3¼mm (No 10/US 3) needles and M, slip 4 sts from right front holder onto a needle, turn, moss st 4.

Cont in moss st **at the same time** inc one st at inside edge on next 7 rows then every foll alt row until there are 21 sts. Cont straight until shaped edge fits along shaped edge of front to shoulder, ending at straight edge.
Shape Collar
Next 2 rows Moss st 12, turn, sl 1, moss st to end.
Moss st 6 rows.
Rep last 8 rows until the shorter edge fits halfway across back neck.
Cast off.

LEFT COLLAR
With wrong side facing, using 3¼mm (No 10/US 3) needles and M, slip 4 sts from left front holder onto a needle, turn, moss st 4. Complete to match right collar.

TO MAKE UP
Join back seam of collar. Sew collar to neck edge. Sew on sleeves. Sew pocket linings in place. Join side and sleeve seams. Sew in zip.

Key
 Cream | Fuchsia Pink
Pale Blue | Main Colour (M)
Stone | Light Pink
Red

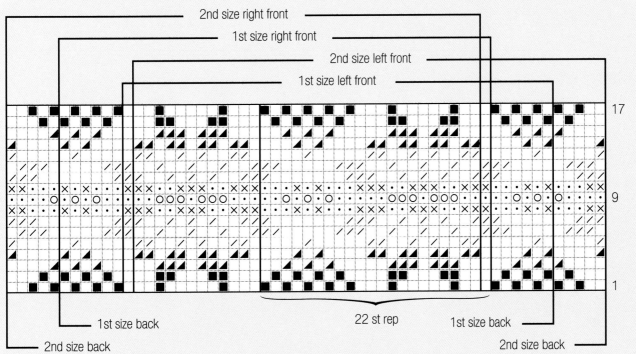

Zipped Scottie Dog Jacket

MATERIALS
Jacket 4(5:6) 100g balls of Novita Isoveli In Main Colour (M).
1(1:1) ball each of same in Red (B) and Black (C).
Pair each of 5½mm (No 5/US 9) and 6mm (No 4/US 10) knitting needles.
30(30:35)cm/12(12:14)in open-ended zip.

MEASUREMENTS

To fit age	2-3	3-4	4-5	years
Actual chest measurement	80	88	92	cm
	31½	34½	36¼	in
Length	40	42	46	cm
	15¾	16½	18	in
Sleeve length	23	25	30	cm
	9	9¾	11¾	in

TENSION
16 sts and 22 rows to 10cm/4in square over st st on 6mm (No 4/US 10) needles.

ABBREVIATIONS
See page 7.

NOTE
Read chart from right to left on right side rows and from left to right on wrong side rows. When working in pattern, strand yarn not in use loosely across wrong side to keep fabric elastic.

BACK
With 5½mm (No 5/US 9) needles and B, cast on 66(70:74) sts.
1st and 3rd sizes only
1st row P2, * k2, p2; rep from * to end.
2nd row K2, * p2, k2; rep from * to end.
2nd size only
1st row K2, * p2, k2; rep from * to end.
2nd row P2, * k2, p2; rep from * to end.
Both sizes
Rep last 2 rows 3 times more, inc 0(2:2) sts evenly across last row. 66(72:76) sts.
Change to 6mm (No 4/US 10) needles and M.
Beg with a k row, work in st st until back measures 40(42:46)cm/15¾(16½:18)in from beg, ending with a p row.
Shape Shoulders
Cast off 11(12:12) sts at beg of next 2 rows and 11(12:13) sts at beg of foll 2 rows.
Cast off rem 22(24:26) sts.

POCKET LININGS (make 2)
With 6mm (No 4/US 10) needles and M, cast on 17 sts.
Beg with a k row, work in st st for 23 rows.

Leave these sts on a holder.

LEFT FRONT
With 5½mm (No 5/US 9) needles and B, cast on 35(37:39) sts.
1st and 3rd sizes only
1st row P2, * k2, p2; rep from * to last 5 sts, k5.
2nd row K3, * p2, k2; rep from * to end.
2nd size only
1st row K2, * p2, k2; rep from * to last 7 sts, p2, k5.
2nd row K3, * p2, k2; rep from * to last 2 sts, p2.
Both sizes
Rep last 2 rows 3 times more.
Change to 6mm (No 4/US 10) needles.
Working 3 sts at front edge in B and garter st and loosely twisting yarns tog at back of work to prevent a hole, cont as follows:
Next row Using M, k to last 3 sts, k3B.
Next row K3B, using M, p to end.
Rep last 2 rows once more.
Next row K11(12:13)M, work across first row of Chart 1, k6(7:8)M, k3B.
Next row K3B, p6(7:8)M, work across second row of Chart 1, p11(12:13)M.
Work a further 12 rows as set.
Next row Using M, k to last 3 sts, k3B.
Next row K3B, using M, p to end.
Next row Using M, k9(10:11), p17, k6(7:8), k3B.
Next row K3B, using M, p to end.
Rep last 2 rows once more.
Place Pocket
Next row Using M, k9(10:11), cast off 17 sts purlwise, k next 5(6:7) sts, k3B.
Next row K3B, using M, p6(7:8), p across sts of pocket lining, p9(10:11).
Cont straight until front measures 32(33:37)cm/12½(13:14½)in from beg, ending with a wrong-side row.
Shape Neck
Next row Using M, k to last 3 sts, turn, leaving these sts on a safety pin.
Dec one st at neck edge on every row until 22(24:25) sts rem.
Cont without further shaping until front measures same as Back to shoulder, ending at side edge.
Shape Shoulder
Cast off 11(12:12) sts at beg of next row.
Work 1 row.
Cast off rem 11(12:13) sts.

RIGHT FRONT
With 5½mm (No 5/US 9) needles and B, cast on 35(37:39) sts.
1st and 3rd sizes only
1st row K5, p2, * k2, p2; rep from * to end.
2nd row K2, * p2, k2; rep from * to last 5 sts, p2, k3.
2nd size only
1st row K5, * p2, k2; rep from * to end.

2nd row P2, * k2, p2; rep from * to last 3 sts, k3.
Both sizes
Rep last 2 rows 3 times more.
Change to 6mm (No 4/US 10) needles.
Working 3 front edge sts in B and garter st, cont as follows:
Next row K3B, using M, k to end.
Next row Using M, p to last 3 sts, k3B.
Rep last 2 rows once more.
Next row K3B, using M, k6(7:8), work across first row of Chart 2, k11(12:13)M.
Next row Using M, p11(12:13), work across second row of Chart 2, p6(7:8)M, k3B.
Work a further 12 rows as set.
Next row K3B, using M, k to end.
Next row Using M, p to last 3 sts, k3B.
Next row K3B, using M, k6(7:8), p17, k9(10:11).
Next row Using M, p to last 3 sts, k3B.
Rep last 2 rows once more.
Place Pocket
Next row K3B, using M, k6(7:8), cast off 17 sts purlwise, k to end.
Next row Using M, p9(10:11), p across sts of pocket lining, p6(7:8), k3B.
Cont straight until front measures 32(33:37)cm/12½(13:14½)in from beg, ending with a wrong-side row.
Shape Neck
Next row K3B, leave these sts on a safety pin, patt to end.
Dec one st at neck edge on every row until 22(24:25) sts rem.

Cont without further shaping until front measures same as Back to shoulder, ending at side edge.
Shape Shoulder
Cast off 11(12:12) sts at beg of next row.
Work 1 row.
Cast off rem 11(12:13) sts.

SLEEVES
With 5½mm (No 5/US 9) needles and B, cast on 30(30:34) sts.
1st row K2, * p2, k2; rep from * to end.
2nd row P2, * k2, p2; rep from * to end.
Rep last 2 rows 3(4:5) times more, inc 6 sts on last row. 36(36:40) sts.
Change to 6mm (No 4/US 10) needles and M.
Beg with a k row, work in st st, inc one st at each end of the 3rd and every foll 4th row until there are 54(58:64) sts.
Cont straight until sleeve measures 23(25:30)cm/9(9¾:11¾)in from beg, ending with a p row.
Cast off.

LEFT COLLAR
With right side facing and using 5½mm (No 5/US 9) needles and B, k across 3 sts on left front band.
K 1 row.
Cont in garter st **at the same time** inc one st at each end of the next and 2 foll 4th rows.
K 2 rows.
Work 6 rows C, 6 rows B and 6 rows C, then cont in B, working

Key

☐ Main Colour (M)

☒ Black (C)

⧀ Red (B)

Chart 1

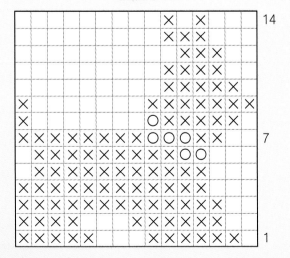

Chart 2

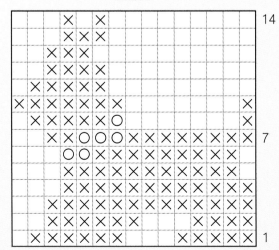

inc as set until there are 23 sts, ending right side of jacket and wrong side of collar facing.

Shape Collar

** Next 2 rows K12, sl 1, turn, k to end.

K 4 rows **.

Rep from ** to ** 4 times.

Cast off.

RIGHT COLLAR

With wrong side facing, using 5½mm (No 5/US 9) needles and B, k across 3 sts on right front band.

Cont in garter st **at the same time** inc one st at each end of the next and 2 foll 4th rows.

K 2 rows.

Work 6 rows C, 6 rows B and 6 rows C, then cont in B, working inc as set until there are 23 sts.

K 1 row, ending right side of jacket and wrong side of collar facing.

Shape Collar

*** Next 2 rows K12, sl 1, turn, k to end.

K 4 rows ***.

Rep from *** to *** 4 times.

Cast off.

TO MAKE UP

Join shoulder seams. Join back seam of collar. Sew collar to neck edge. Sew on sleeves. Sew pocket linings in place. Join side and sleeve seams. Sew in zip.

Striped Silk Top

MATERIALS
2(3:3) 50g balls Jaeger Silk 4 ply in Cream (A).
1 ball each of same in Grey (B) and Red (C).
Pair each of 2¾mm (No 12/US 2) and 3¼mm (No 10/US 3) knitting needles.
3 buttons.

MEASUREMENTS

To fit ages	3	6	12	months
Actual chest measurement	55	60	68	cm
	21½	23½	26¾	in
Length	26	28	32	cm
	10¼	11¼	12¾	in
Sleeve length	14	16	18	cm
	5½	6¼	7	in

TENSION
28 sts and 38 rows to 10cm/4in square over st st on 3¼mm (No10/US 3) needles.

ABBREVIATIONS
See page 7.

BACK
With 2¾mm (No 12/US 2) needles and B, cast on 79(86:97) sts.
K 9 rows.
Change to 3¼mm (No 10/US 3) needles.
Using a separate length of B at each end and twisting yarns tog on wrong side when changing colour, work as follows:
1st row K3B, with A, k to last 3 sts, k3B.
2nd row K3B, with A, p to last 3 sts, k3B
3rd row K3B, with C, k to last 3 sts, k3B.
4th row K3B, with C, p to last 3 sts, k3B
5th row K3B, with A, k to last 3 sts, k3B.
6th row K3B, with A, p to last 3 sts, k3B
Beg with a k row, work in st st and stripe patt of 2 rows B, 2 rows A, 2 rows C and 2 rows A until back measures 23(25:29)cm/9(10:11½)in from beg, ending with a p row.
Shape Neck
Next row K23(25:30) sts, turn and work on this set of sts only.
Work 11 rows in patt, ending with a p row.
Shape Shoulder
Change to 2¾mm (No 12/US 2) needles.
With A, k 3 rows.
Cast off.
With right side facing, slip centre 35(36:37) sts onto a holder, join on yarn, patt to end.
Work 11 rows in patt, ending with a p row.

Shape Shoulder
Change to 2¾mm (No 12/US 2) needles.
With A, k 5 rows.
Cast off.

FRONT
Work as given for Back until 6 rows less have been worked to neck shaping.
Shape Neck
Next row K23(25:30) sts, turn and work on this set of sts only.
Work 17 rows in patt, ending with a p row.
Shape Shoulder
Change to 2¾mm (No 12/US 2) needles.
With A, k 2 rows.
Buttonhole row K4(5:7), k2tog, yf, k9(10:12), yf, k2tog, k6(6:7).
K 2 rows.
Cast off.
With right side facing, slip centre 35(36:37) sts onto a holder, join on yarn, patt to end.
Work 17 rows in patt, ending with a p row.
With A, k 3 rows.
Cast off.

SLEEVES
With 2¾mm (No 12/US 2) needles and B, cast on 34(37:40) sts.
K 9 rows.
Change to 3¼mm (No10/US 3) needles.
Beg with a k row, work in st st and stripe patt of 2 rows A, 2 rows C, 2 rows A and 2 rows B, **at the same time** inc 1 st at each end of every foll 3rd row until there are 60(69:76) sts.
Cont straight until sleeve measures 14(16:18)cm/5½(6¼:7)in from beg, ending with a p row.
Cast off.

NECKBAND
Join right shoulder seam.
With right side facing, using 2¾mm (No 12/US 2) needles and A, pick up and k16 sts down left side of front neck, k35(36:37) sts from front neck, pick up and k14 sts up right side of front neck, k8 sts down right side of back neck, k35(36:37) sts from back neck, pick up and k10 sts up left side of back neck. 118(120:122) sts.
K 1 row.
Buttonhole row K2, k2tog, yf, k10, skpo, k2tog, k31(32:33), skpo, k2tog, k18, skpo, k2tog, k31(32:33), skpo, k2tog, k8.
K 1 row.
Dec row K13, skpo, k2tog, k29(30:31), skpo, k2tog, k16, skpo, k2tog, k29(30:31), skpo, k2tog, k7.
K 1 row.
Dec row K12, skpo, k2tog, k27(28:29), skpo, k2tog, k14, skpo, k2tog, k27(28:29), skpo, k2tog, k6.
K 1 row.
Cast off, dec at corners as before.

TO MAKE UP
Lap buttonhole band over right back button band and catch side edges together. Sew on sleeves. Join side and sleeve seams to top of side slit. Sew on buttons.

YARN SUPPLIERS

Debbie Bliss Yarns
Debbie Bliss's shop
Yarn, kits, ready-to-wear garments,
books and toys are available from
Debbie Bliss's shop:
Debbie Bliss
365 St John Street
London EC1V 4LB
Tel: 020 7833 8255
Fax: 020 7833 3588
Website:
www.debbiebliss.freeserve.co.uk

Head Office
Designer Yarns Ltd
1 Tivoli Place
Ilkley
W Yorks LS29 8SU
Tel: 01943 604123
Fax: 01943 600320

USA
Knitting Fever Inc.
35 Debevoise Avenue
Roosevelt
NY 11575
Tel: (516) 546 3600
Fax: (516) 546 6871

Canada
Diamond Yarn
9697 St Laurent
Montreal
Quebec H3L 2N1
Tel: (514) 386 6188

Diamond Yarn (Toronto)
155 Martin Ross
Unit 3
Toronto
Ontario M3J 2L9
Tel: (416) 736 6111

Novita Yarns
United Kingdom
Designer Yarns Ltd
1 Tivoli Place
Ilkley
W Yorks LS29 8SU
Tel: 01943 604123
Fax: 01943 600320

USA
Knitting Fever Inc.
35 Debevoise Avenue
Roosevelt
NY 11575
Tel: (516) 546 3600
Fax: (516) 546 6871

Canada
Diamond Yarn
9697 St Laurent
Montreal
Quebec H3L 2N1
Tel: (514) 386 6188

Diamond Yarn (Toronto)
155 Martin Ross
Unit 3
Toronto
Ontario M3J 2L9
Tel: (416) 736 6111

Scandinavia
Helsingin Villakehräämö Oy/Novita
Box 59
00211 Helsinki
Finland
Tel: +358 9 6131 76
Fax: +358 9 6131 7700

Baltic Countries
Novita Eesti Oü
Laki 12 A
EE-10621 Tallinn
Estonia
Tel: +372 656 3883
Fax: +372 656 3758

Russia
Law Key Ltd
196247, St Petersburg
Leninsky Pr 160
Russia
Tel: +7 812 295 78 66
Fax: +7 812 118 46 65

Rowan and Jaeger Yarns
United Kingdom
Head office
Rowan Yarns
Green Lane Mill
Holmfirth
West Yorkshire HD7 1RW
Tel: 01484 681 881
Fax: 01484 687 920
E-mail: rowanmail@rowanyarns.co.uk

USA
Rowan USA
5 Northern Boulevard
Amherst
NH 03031
Tel: (603) 886 5041/5043
E-mail: wfibers@aol.com

Canada
Diamond Yarn
9697 St Laurent
Montreal
Quebec H3L 2N1
Tel: (514) 386 6188

Diamond Yarn (Toronto)
155 Martin Ross
Unit 3
Toronto
Ontario M3J 2L9
Tel: (416) 736 6111

Acknowledgments

This book would not have been possible without the invaluable contribution of the following band of dedicated people:

The long suffering knitters: Pat Church, Jane Crowfoot, Jacqui Dunt, Penny Hill, Shirley Kennet, Maisie Lawrence, Frances Wallace, Beryl Salter, Janet Fagan, Dorothy Bayliss, Cynthia Brent.

Jane Crowfoot, who contributed the lovely striped designs.

The models: a big thank you to Amy, Charlie, Grace, Lavinia, Caitlin, Hannah, Brandon, Lola, Max, Nell, Sam, Scarlet, Summer, Natalie, Ciara and Yaiza.

A huge thank you to Marilyn Wilson, who checked the patterns.

Craig Fordham and Jemima Mills, the photographer and stylist who not only created the beautiful look but also the perfect atmosphere to work in.

Rob, the photographer's assistant, for making us laugh on the shoot.

Denise Bates, my editor, for her unfailing support of my projects.

Christine Wood – thank you for the beautiful design of this book.

Emma Callery, for her great attention to detail in the editing.

Ciara Lunn, editorial assistant – just perfect.

Heather Jeeves, my wonderful agent.